Against the Grain

Against the Grain

Writings of a Sceptical Optimist

SIMON JENKINS

JOHN MURRAY
Albemarle Street, London

A catalogue record for this book is available
from the British Library

ISBN 0-7195-5570-1

Typeset in Linotron 11½/13½pt Times
by Rowland Phototypesetting Ltd.,
Bury St Edmunds, Suffolk
Printed and bound in Great Britain at
the University Press, Cambridge

For
Edward

CONTENTS

vii

CONTENTS

And on to Other Things

CONTENTS

PREFACE

ESSAY, PIECE, column, article, there is no accepted noun for a short passage of prose. Most of the pieces in this collection began as columns, almost all in *The Times*. But the staccato of a column is not always right for a book. The eye treats the narrow width of newsprint more harshly than it does the page of a book. Newspaper readers demand topicality and immediacy. These articles are longer than columns. They are meant to adhere to Virginia Woolf's 'controlling principle of all writing, which is to give pleasure.' But they are all fashioned to a purpose, to persuade the reader of a point of view.

I believe that the column, much in vogue in today's journalism, is in direct line of descent from the tracts and sermons of the seventeenth-century propagandists. Bacon said of his essays that they should 'begin in doubt and end in certainty'. That is a sound columnist's maxim. The essayist may be a prima donna and the columnist a balladeer. But both have evolved hand in hand with the development of popular journalism. They cannot deny their kinship. Both dress up in style, like to spice their conversation with humour and have a compulsion to moralize. Both either engage the mind of the reader or are so much waste paper.

These pieces are gathered into three groups. The first are primarily political. As every journalist knows, nothing deteriorates as fast as politics. Its controversies come and go with such speed that only a blurr often remains on the lens of even the most immediate commentator. I have confined myself to arguing against received wisdom only where that wisdom and my argument are likely to survive for some time, as over the fate of the Liberal Party or the unpopularity of prime ministers.

The second group of pieces concerns social and environmental controversies where again I find myself going against the grain, but where I hope a more lasting dialogue is possible. The third group offers a less strident and more eccentric comment on the Britain of the 1990s. I end with that troubled troubadour, the nightingale. God preserve him, along with hedges, phone boxes, watercolours, St Francis of Assisi, the works of George Eliot and all the denizens of Pandora's box, including Lady Hope.

I would like to thank *The Times* for permission to reproduce those pieces that are similar to ones that appeared in its pages. Of them and of the rest, I can only quote the happy advice of the Edwardian critic, Maurice Hewlitt: 'Go turn your column into a maypole, and pace out your dedicatory dance!'

Aspects of Politics

1

MEMOIR WARS

THIS WAS to be the killer memoir. For months we knew it was coming. The tiddlers had occupied the pools. A few trout had glided through and disappeared. But now a menacing shape was moving upstream, its dorsal swirling the surface. Spectators watched aghast. The beast's navigation appeared deranged. Death awaited it in the shallows, but even in these cramped waters it was lethal.

Margaret Thatcher's autobiography of her years in Downing Street was presold as 'the whole dirt'. It would at last reveal 'her side' of a story, a story that had already been widely told. Her government had yielded a rich harvest of self-exculpatory memoirs, richer even than the Wilson government. Some had been meticulously anodyne, such as those of the grandees. Lord Whitelaw was horrified when a friend congratulated him on being so 'interesting'. It was the last thing he had meant to be, much to the chagrin of the *Sunday Times* which had contracted to publish extracts. The paper had to send a reporter to try and squeeze more juice out of the old man. It failed.

A few devout Thatcherites felt obliged to act as her forerunners, preparing the ground, swatting a few lesser enemies. These volumes were either tedious, in the case of Sir Norman

3

Fowler, Lord Tebbit and Lord Parkinson, or mildly enlightening, such as that by Lord Ridley. The dispossessed of Thatcherism had other motives. They wanted to get their own back on their boss or at least on some of their colleagues. In this category I would put the works of Lord Pym, Lord Prior, Sir Ian Gilmour and Kenneth Baker, and on a higher plane the vast and erudite tome of Lord Lawson. Some of these lifted the curtain to reveal an occasional pool of blood. They were under terrible pressure from their publishers, each peddling the narcotic of revenge in the hope of securing a gagging writ or a letter of complaint from the Cabinet Secretary.

The authors would shudder at the indignity of it all. They were under oath as privy councillors. The cabinet rules clearly lay down that ministers must not reveal in their memoirs the content of any discussion that reflects on the conduct of a colleague, let alone a civil servant. One reason is that the victim might be induced to hit back, which would be a dreadful thing. Most authors now yield to this temptation. While a cabinet secret is merely a cabinet secret, a book is Milton's precious lifeblood of a master spirit. A book must be sold, at whatever cost to the good conduct of Her Majesty's government. Besides, 'rightly to be great is . . . to find quarrel in a straw when honour's at the stake.' One must always ensure a safe place for one's honour in history – in advance of possible counterclaims.

All this began under Lord Wilson, with the end of the cabinet as a private dining club with unwritten rules. Cabinet secrecy collapsed under the pens of Richard Crossman, Barbara Castle and Tony Benn. They complained that Wilson himself breached secrecy by using his press secretary to convey his own gloss on a cabinet debate to the parliamentary lobby after each meeting. If one cabinet member broke ranks, others felt duty bound to 'set the record straight'. When we turn up the index of history, we all hope to see our name in print, however passing the reference. With ministerial careers ever more abbreviated under Margaret Thatcher, and the press office conduit ever more abused, the prospect was of cabinet arguments appearing in the columns of newspapers at near dictation speed.

After the Crossman diaries appeared in the 1970s, cabinets became ever more open. The same process affected Parliament in the eighteenth century. Reporting was prohibited and a pamphleteer was even jailed for suggesting that there were 'two sides' to a debate in the House. Samuel Johnson was among many to breach this secrecy, albeit by writing up debates as if they were fictional events. This is now happening to the cabinet. As it becomes a more public forum so, like the House of Commons, its discussions become less significant to the conduct of government.

Enthusiasts for open government welcome this. The more leaks, the more cabinet memoirs, the better for democracy. Open up the innards of government, and the public will be the better able to hold ministers to account, the better able to exercise a direct influence over decisions. If we cannot ourselves kick politicians where it hurts, at least we can enjoy watching them do it to each other. But where to draw the line? In Washington, the disclosure of documents from every nook and cranny of government is now *de rigueur*. The destruction even of manuscript notepads or doodles is banned lest some court should want to make hay with them. Some participants in American government seem to regard their term in office as merely a preparation for 'the book'. Round them circle a ready pack of journalists, purveyors of instant history. Since the Watergate affair, history has come to be not what happened but what the least discreet, or more frightened, official said to the first Boswell to walk into his room and set a microphone on his desk.

I have read no more extraordinary book on modern government than David Stockman's *The Triumph of Politics*, a sarcastic title. It relates Stockman's time as President Reagan's budget director. The portrait of Mr Reagan and his defence secretary, Caspar Weinberger, playing Russian roulette with the public sector deficit over defence spending is enthralling and terrifying. It is a story of how raw democracy can destroy fiscal responsibility. In one sense, every democrat should read it and be warned. But I would never trust Stockman with a confidence if my life depended on it. A similarly indiscreet exercise was Strobe Talbot's *Deadly Gambits*, an account of the arms control battle between Richard Perle at the Pentagon and Richard Burt at the State Department in the early 1980s. This was a gripping account of the struggles of hawks and doves in the dying years of the Cold War. It left no stone unturned, no conversation unrecorded or unrecalled by the participants. It was clear that Talbot was able to play each character off against the other by going back and forth between them. And all this while they were still in government service.

The habit is catching. The 1991 Gulf War yielded graphic accounts of the rivalry between commanders, of the sort that in the Second World War had to await the deaths of those involved and posthumous papers and diaries. No such restraint operates today. The Gulf War instantly gave us General Norman Schwarzkopf's *It Doesn't Take a Hero*, General Sir Peter de la Billière's *Storm Command* and Bob Woodward's *The Commanders*. Few confidences appear to have been respected, presumably excluding those that put the authors in a bad light. Most wartime generals develop a loathing for politicians: politicians want speed when caution is needed and offer only indecision when speed is required. Since generals usually tell better war stories than politicians, their books sell better. Woe betide a defence minister who sends a literary general to war.

The question is whether the growth of kiss-and-tell memoirs written soon after a climactic event affects the behaviour, perhaps even the decisions, of the participants in public affairs. I cannot see it otherwise. The confidences necessary for compromise between colleagues must be distorted. Some ministers say that this is not so. Such is the pressure of events and so great are the issues at stake that the last thing a minister has time to do is wonder how his contribution will look to history. I wonder. Reading Strobe Talbot's book I felt those involved were pre-enacting the script of the film of the book that was already in their imagina-

6

tions. Why therefore concede any point, why admit any compromise? Stick to your first position and with luck you will be portrayed by Robert Redford.

Time was when neither politicians nor officials knifed each other in the back on retirement. Generals did that sort of thing – Allenbrook, Wavell, Montgomery – but their victories were behind them and they had nothing more to guard but their reputations. Old soldiers did not fade away, they fought on through the columns of their memoirs and the letters page of *The Times*. Other public servants do not on the whole breach confidences. Diplomats produce fluffy collections of diplomatic anecdotes. Lloyd George's secretary, Tom Jones, published late in life his remarkable diary and letters, as did Churchill's secretary, Lord Colville, and his doctor, Lord Moran. These were real insights into their subject's public and private lives, but appeared after a dignified lapse of time. No senior civil servant that I can recall has rushed into print to relate the antics of serving ministers, gripping though these would surely be. Officials do not go public on what happened to the advice they offer to ministers. Equally, they rely on ministers not to comment on that advice.

Lord Lawson's memoir of his time as Chancellor of the Exchequer stirred strong protest from the Cabinet Office in advance of its publication. He was rumoured to have indicated in some detail the advice he was given, and the sense or nonsense of that advice. Many of those who gave it were serving his successor. He resisted the pressure for censorship. In the event, the comments on senior Treasury officials were less than devastating. But another hole was made in the once-impregnable wall of discretion. More devastating were Alan Clark's diaries. His account of his relations (in every sense) with secretaries, officials and foreign diplomats was more than unkind. It breached confidentiality, etiquette and even gallantry. But at least Clark spared nobody, not even himself.

The Thatcher book is extraordinary in having been hyped quite specifically as revenge. She was out to murder her foes. This would not be the story of a government, the history of a decade, the old chief turning the diary pages with a smile and a pair of rose-tinted glasses. Such conceits were for old fogies. This was to be the flashing knife. And just to make the point the book was not issued in advance for review. Those who intended to comment in print on its 862 pages would have to do so at the same time as the readers of the massive *Sunday Times* serialization.

Never has hype been so overdone. Lady Thatcher does not murder her enemies, she sends them to sleep with great chunks of edited official documents. The knifings read as casual inserts. The author kept no diary, except during the Falklands War, and the recollection was thus of notes and minutes from the files with her characteristically terse comments in the margin. There was to be no dialogue and she seemed uninterested in the colour or human interest of power. Instead the reader is hit with a 40-page review of the miners' strike, a 25-page critique of domestic rates, notes on all 24 European Council meetings. Much was clearly not written by the author and the 'memoirs team' as it was known was seldom allowed to relax. Clothes, food, friends, laughter or tears, holidays are rarely allowed to intrude on the onward march of the revolution. Indeed as I read this huge book I began to hallucinate. Those interminable speeches by Brezhnev or Castro must have seemed like this to their listeners. A book of 862 pages is megalomania.

There are a moments of self-awareness. Lady Thatcher admits she could be domineering but adds, 'My experience is that a group of men sitting round a table like little better than their own voice.' Anyone who sat at the same table as Lady Thatcher could be forgiven a grim laugh at that. 'My style of chairmanship nonplussed some colleagues who knew their briefs a good deal less well than I did,' she continues with characteristic self-deprecation. Foreign leaders are no better treated. Arriving at an Athens summit she records her suspicion that the French and German leaders had empty tables in front of them. Hers was heavy with annotated briefs on agricultural support and budgetary stabilizers. The others had surely 'not mastered their briefs . . . and this turned out to be the case.' She is relentless with others whatever their position. The German Chancellor, Helmut Kohl, desperate at one point to soothe relations, invites her to his home, greeting her with a beaming smile and warm Rhineland hospitality. She retorts, 'I instantly took him to task, deploying all the arguments for a credible short-range nuclear deterrent and for sticking to agreed Nato decisions.' Small wonder, she smugly records, that the man soon became 'deeply uncomfortable'. She seems to have been completely un-housetrained.

The Thatcher memoirs set a new standard in open government, of a sort. The former Prime Minister objected to any lapse in cabinet loyalty by a minister, yet boasts her technique of 'using public statements to push reluctant colleagues further than they would go' in pursuing her policies. She tested Foreign Office loyalty close to breaking point opposing German reunification. This developed into fiercely anti-German remarks made to all and sundry. These were not government policy or discussed in cabinet. Anti-Germanism was a personal prejudice elevated to a one-woman crusade. In the memoirs she admits her 'unambiguous failure' to impede the path of German reunification. She also records her effort to enlist President Mitterrand to the cause at a series of private meetings. The news of these briefly electrified German politics at the time of publication. A British leader disclosing the most sensitive of diplomatic exchanges when the other parties to them were still in power must be, at best, unethical. Mitterrand was wise to resist her blandishments – and to tell the Germans he had done so.

Never was a prime minister so obviously 'first among equals', their equality only displayed when they ousted her in a series of personal encounters, like the murder of Julius Caesar. To her, colleagues were either blindly loyal, like Lord Whitelaw, or inadequate and potentially devious. All were below stairs. Of 83 pictures of Lady Thatcher with world leaders such as Reagan and Gorbachev not one shows her with Lord Howe or Lord Lawson or Douglas Hurd or indeed any personality of her regime other than the party chairman at election time. There is not one photograph identifying the members of any of her cabinets. This supremacist approach to government is carried on in the one light relief offered by the book, the casual side-swipes at 'colleagues'. These are startling to read and certainly were to their victims. During a television documentary made of the book, the producers asked her colleagues to comment on her reign, which they did with proper dignity. They were then read the references to them from the embargoed text of the book and offered the chance of a second 'take'. Some were stunned, others gleefully accepted.

Her two greatest foes were apparently the two men who strove so valiantly to uphold the Thatcherite crusade through long years of struggle, Sir Geoffrey Howe and Nigel Lawson. Apart from an occasional 'superb' or 'talented' they are eventually dismissed as foolish, bilious and treacherous. Other cabinet members lack even such dainty morsels. If she thought so little of Francis Pym, Ian Gilmour, Jim Prior and John Gummer one wonders why she appointed them all to such high office. Even if she felt the national interest to be served by breaking the confidences of government, some dis-cretion might surely have been extended to the demeanour of friends at the moment when she chose to execute them, often after allowing their impending demise to leak to the press beforehand. Gilmour went 'huffily', Soames was 'angry', while the 'ineffective and left-leaning' Carlisle went with 'courtesy and good humour'. The author recognizes no right to privacy.

The central charge levied by Lord Lawson in his memoir is that Lady Thatcher was at best a fair-weather Thatcherite. She was a closet wet, expecting her ministers to go out and fight the corporatist dragons but deserting them when the going got tough. Lawson cited tax reform, spending cuts to defence and law and order, radical reform of health, housing, transport. Hers were the instincts of a suburban politician rather than an ideological crusader. All the rest was rhetoric.

I suspect that all Lawson was doing was stating the obvious. A prime minister's job is to be the ultimate politician, the fount of compromise in government. In their Treasury bas-tion, Howe and Lawson could afford to be valiant for truth.

They did not have to carry the electoral can. When in 1990 Lady Thatcher admitted defeat on the European exchange rate mechanism – to John Major as Chancellor – she confessed 'eventually I had to . . . I had too few allies to go on resisting.' On domestic policy she admits she was 'a Fabian not a Napoleon'. The book is littered with strategic withdrawals, on the miners and dockers, on pensions and education reform, on public spending year in year out. What I find most extraordinary about Lady Thatcher is that she maintained the energy to keep driving on, to sustain forward momentum even when she lacked the 'six good men and true' fighting at her side that she claimed she needed.

The Thatcher memoirs are not really history, although her culling of cabinet documents and her presumably partial account of them will give historians a little meat on which to chew. I regard them more as Lady Thatcher furiously waving her flag in history's face, daring it to defy her. The task for historians is to disentangle the truth from the dross. Instant memoirs are not works of research. They are not even an attempt at a 'first rough draft' of history, although Lawson on occasions comes near it. They are an attempt to bias the draft before somebody else writes it. Historical truth is an ever shifting desert. It is charted more accurately when viewed from some distance. One of the best such 'drafts' was Selwyn Lloyd's memoir on Suez, written at the end of his life in protest against other variably inaccurate accounts of his actions.

As a journalist I have a professional interest in disclosure. I believe in freedom of speech and publication. In pursuit of that I will gladly induce every politician to reveal all, to the illumination of the public and the education of future leaders. But I also hold what may seem a contradictory belief, that the result of ministers capitulating to publishers' blandishments is damaging to good government. It pushes the real argument of public administration, the pressuring, the horse-trading, back into the shadows. In Washington, freedom of information has led the executive to retreat into cabals and coteries, to what Henry Kissinger and Oliver North termed

their 'back channels'. The formal conduits of crisis management become so clogged with mistrust that only 'buddies'
who can rely totally on each other's confidence are admitted
to the inner circle of decision. Kitchen cabinets have been
the curse of British government. Indiscretion enhances their
role.

There must be a virtue in a democratically elected executive
preserving privacy in reaching its decisions. Its members must
feel they can argue free of the fear that anybody worsted in
the argument will rush to the first publisher or editor to come
his way. Otherwise intrigue will feed on intrigue. Government
will become a real-time rehearsal for a subsequent fictional
drama. Perhaps cabinet membership should include a con-
tractual commitment not to write a memoir for ten years after
leaving office. Clearly the club needs new rules. Government,
as Bagehot said, is meant to be a dull business, the duller the
better.

But I should miss the memoir wars.

2

ONE COUNTRY:
TWO SAINTS

I LOVE South Africa and have done so ever since my first visit in 1977. For years it was a closet love, conducted beneath the carapace of journalism. Each visit would be to pursue a story, an interview, a survey. I would grab a day or two and sneak off to a mountain or a beach, visit a friend, talk to all and sundry. Every journalist needs one 'far country', a political second home, a place from which to view Britain from time to time. When I returned to London and said I had been in South Africa, I enjoyed watching people take the instinctive step backwards as if fearing contamination. They would ascertain whether I was a native or sympathizer, someone who might communicate a germ of political incorrectness to them.

I believed that apartheid was obnoxious and held no plausible vision of a stable future. But I could never view it as qualitatively more obnoxious than a dozen other ideologies then prevailing round the globe, half of them elsewhere in Africa. The regimes of Nigeria, Rwanda, Ethiopia and Zaire were behaving towards ethnic minorities, and even majorities, in a manner that could only be excused by those who felt black governments need not behave as well as white ones. To that racist doctrine I could not subscribe. Multiracial nations are seldom stable. Nobody has any model constitution to offer them. But in South Africa's case I did feel that the political classes on both sides of the racial divide might yet find their own way out of the morass if left to draw their own map. Ostracism and sanctions, in themselves empty weapons of political aggression, had at least the virtue of *laissez-faire*. South Africa could go about finding its own salvation in its own way.

Hence my delight when in 1990 the Afrikaner Nationalist government embarked on the road of change with the release of Nelson Mandela from prison. That delight increased when in 1994 the road reached its most important way-station, a proper democratic election. I had guessed it might take five years. It took just over four. I have no doubt that the reason lay in the specific qualities of the two leaders involved. I am no Tolstoyan determinist. South Africa's course to democracy was in no way inevitable and came near to disaster. But a peaceful election and a peaceful transfer of power took place. They did so against all prediction, not least a worldwide liberal conviction that only bloody revolution would dislodge the whites from power. Here surely was an instant in political history when the character of individuals patently conditioned the passage of events.

In the middle of the April 1994 election campaign the then state president, F. W. de Klerk, remarked bitterly that 'this is not a coronation, it is an election'. He knew he was wrong. The only suspense was over the balance of power in the national and provincial assemblies. The election was a coronation and there was no doubt who would be king. But who, I wondered, most deserved sainthood? Of Mandela's sanctity there appeared no doubt. He was not just the charismatic leader of a dispossessed community. Even before his release from prison in 1990 he exerted astonishing authority over South Africa's whites and blacks alike. As he emerged from a quarter-century of incarceration, he was calm, conciliatory, above all sensible. He was a lawyer. He respected the rule of law and knew, like that other South African lawyer, Mahatma Gandhi, that it held the only guarantee of freedom. His constant theme, 'We must all work together', was not just a

14

cliché. It guided his conduct through four years of near-intolerable argument and pressure.

He should have broken under the strain. He was 72 and a sick man at the time of his release. He seemed unsteady and had to endure the awful discovery that his wife, Winnie, was not what he had fondly imagined. Dealing with the politics of the African National Congress was no easier. Split between exiled and underground factions, between militants and pacifists, between capitalists and communists, it was a caricature of a liberation movement. The Zulu people and Chief Buthelezi's Inkatha Freedom Party nagged at his flank all the time. Mandela had to blow hot and cold throughout the constitutional negotiations to keep his own people on-side. Sometimes the game seemed hopeless, as after the Boipatong killings and the revelations that the police had been helping Inkatha to attack ANC supporters. Mandela seemed constantly on the brink of losing control of the process. In early 1992 the negotiations were temporarily suspended. Pessimists said this was the moment they had predicted, when South Africa would retreat into guerrilla war and armed oppression. Yet it did not happen.

Mandela's authority was of character rather than of word or deed. He carried with him the integrity of his trial and the Rivonia speech, and the fact of his imprisonment. He was indecisive, a common feature of African politicians though not necessarily a disadvantageous one. The politics of that continent are dilatory. Decisions that have emerged from a group consensus are more valid, and more acceptable, than those imposed by decisive leadership. With able lieutenants in Cyril Ramaphosa, Thabo Mbeki and, until his murder, Chris Hani, Mandela was able to keep his rambling coalition together through the four-year interregnum. Courteous, conservative, a good listener, he knew that constitutions must be built on rocks of consent, even interim ones. White rule in South Africa was always constitutional. Its ending had to be no less constitutional. Political apartheid was respected by all sides until the moment when a new president and assembly were sworn in May 1994.

Yet Mandela could be accommodating because, in any true democracy, he and his cohorts could not lose. The black electorate was not likely to desert him in his hour of triumph. For him democracy would mean coronation. President de Klerk's whites were not so reliable. Throughout the 1980s, they had shifted and argued and split. They had done so half to preserve apartheid, half to preserve the good things of white rule against the inevitable advance of black power. Their leaders had searched for middle ways. The 'survival ethic' was on their lips at every seminar. Anything would be better than for South Africa to go the way of black Africa to the north. For some that anything meant even a qualified black democracy, for others it meant armed resistance. But the odds were that at some point in the 1990s enough whites would say, so far and no further, and stop progress in its tracks.

When de Klerk assumed the leadership of the National Party and held what proved to be the last apartheid election in 1989, he seemed condemned to the most miserable of roles. He would preside over the collapse of Africa's longest running and most prosperous tribal oligarchy, collapse not into democracy but into anarchy. This was no Kenya or Rhodesia. The whites of South Africa could well have held onto a measure of real power well into the next century. If communist parties could keep half the world enslaved for half a century, then a capitalist minority regime certainly had a decade left in its locker. There was an array of more or less plausible options on offer, including a much-touted confederalism that left whites with national control but over decentralized black provinces. There was the 'Zulu card' granting *de facto* regional independence to Natal. There were fancy franchises, like those attempted in post-colonial states to the north.

None of this happened. The sudden loss of the whites' will to rule remains a mystery. Neither fear of a black uprising nor, certainly, any external pressure through sanctions can claim credit. I believe the reason was a moral collapse, a realization on the part of whites that, with the ending of

16

apartheid, there was no longer any ideological justification for denying the blacks democracy. White South Africans always believed themselves to be democrats. English-speakers, represented by the United and then Progressive Federal parties, had long yearned for another route than apartheid. In the 1980s, Afrikaners came to the same conclusion. One of their leading philosophers, Willie van der Esterhuyse, pointed out that the Afrikaner is nothing if not a rationalist. He needs a coherent creed by which to live. White supremacy was not enough. Even Verwoerd had to elevate apartheid or 'separate development' into a coherent ideology. He presented it as a democratic reform to legitimize the removal of blacks out of white areas to homelands in which they could vote. When this policy failed, another had to be found. Politicians, diplomats, editors, novelists, clergymen, businessmen, all plunged into a decade of restless self-examination. It was a process that recalled seventeenth-century England. To a visitor from abroad, it was mesmerizing.

President de Klerk offered the simplest of answers, democracy, the whole democracy and nothing but democracy. I recall meeting him at his Cape home in Hermanus in 1991, early in the constitutional negotiating process. He was sitting in a modest cottage between the hills and the sea, protected by just a white wall and a couple of guards. I had met him once before, when he seemed a colourless minister of no obvious distinction. Now he surprised me by his radicalism. There would never be in South Africa, he said, a 'fancy white franchise like the British used when they left this continent'. All South Africans had to be politically equal. There could be no privileged voters. Whatever else might be done to the constitution to safeguard minorities, it would not be through loaded voting. I wondered at the daring of this gamble. Yet within a year of our conversation, de Klerk had won a whites-only referendum for full black democracy, with Mandela in support. Virtue favoured the bold. I can think of no other nation in which an ethnic minority has voluntarily handed over power so completely to a majority, with no hope of recovery.

De Klerk was the man who presided over this process. He suffered the most maniacal dissidents in his own security forces, men whose hand could be seen in successive bombings and shootings right up to election night. He had to face increasingly bitter attacks on his Afrikaner credentials from the far right. Andries Treurnicht and Constand Viljoen, two former colleagues in government, broke away to found 'volk' parties. Treurnicht's Conservatives became the official opposition in 1989 and might have been within sight of power under less implausible leadership. De Klerk realized that there comes a moment along the path of change when caution and delay are the enemies of success. He had to reassure whites that he was in control, even of the process of diluting and ultimately losing power. He had to be the figure of stability, the calm voice in the midst of the maelstrom.

Real crisis came early in 1992 when the multi-party talks collapsed and harsh words were required of each other by both Mandela and de Klerk. Both leaders returned to their base camps and communed with their supporters. They had to recharge their leadership batteries with tribal consent, or lose the capacity to compromise. Either might have failed. Mandela's ANC militants were nervous of being outflanked by the Pan-African Congress and by youth leaders in the townships. De Klerk's critics were on every side, most severe on the right. Both men contrived to reassert their authority and recommence the talks. After the crisis de Klerk's negotiators conceded point after point to the ANC on the interim constitution and transitional cabinet. But de Klerk never sacrificed his authority to the process of concession. He sensed that his one weapon against white despair was white dignity. He and his colleagues were granting power to the blacks, not having it snatched from them. Let dignity slip and the dogs of civil war would run wild.

The de Klerk charisma is more subdued than that of Mandela, more homely. His smile is natural and his manner of speaking matter-of-fact. Mandela has an episcopalian bearing and manner. His English is stilted, as if not his first tongue (though it is). When required to 'toy-toy' on stage during the

18

election campaign, immaculate in grey suit, Mandela did so with the same shy condescension as de Klerk showed when being garlanded by girls at a Soweto school. Not for him the vain ranting of Desmond Tutu, the Cape Town bishop. Tutu's image was an old familiar, that of an African politician on the make. Mandela seemed more like an English governor-general. For most whites, the exchange of Mandela for Tutu was an immense relief.

Both Mandela and de Klerk enjoy that boon in politics of being able to display, behind whatever mask the times may require, a simple and direct niceness. When in 1992 they said hard things about each other, the anger was genuine but 'ring-fenced'. When at their final television debate during the election campaign, Mandela went across and shook de Klerk warmly by the hand, many South Africans burst into tears. 'How could we be so lucky as to have those two men as leaders?' said Afrikaner friends of mine. After all they had done, how could they be so fortunate? As the old saying went, surely God was a South African.

That saying used to be wheeled out whenever some new catastrophe appeared to loom over South Africa, only to be repelled by some good fortune. Fortune might take the form of a gold price surge, or civil war in a front-line state, or the end of a drought, or just a sublime sunset over Table Bay. But fortune certainly attended the moment of South Africa's transition from oligarchy to democracy. One reason, I firmly believe, is that the transition was kept internal. Apart from futile interventions by the Commonwealth's 'eminent persons' group, and at the last minute by Henry Kissinger and Lord Carrington, there were no arbitrators or peace-seekers or conciliators. There was no high-profile shuttle diplomacy. There were no promises of a show on the White House lawn or millions in aid to a Swiss bank account. Nobody but South Africans would get credit for bringing democracy to South Africa (though many outsiders tried). Nobody but South Africans would be blamed if it failed.

Perhaps the circumstance of history does throw up particular leaders. By 1989 P. W. Botha had reached the limit of his ability to compromise on constitutional reform. The Afrikaner National Party selected as leader a man who was both a born compromiser and its most deft politician. It rejected the unsophisticated but liberal Pik Botha, the showy Magnus Malan, the studious Gerrit Viljeon. Its instinct was that only de Klerk would keep the trust of the whites in doing 'whatever was now necessary'. On the other side of the equation, when Mandela came out of prison, the ANC factions were drawn to his leadership as the one guarantee of unity. The young turks who might have seized power from the returning exiles and prisoners – the ANC had no internal democracy – sensed that this would have been a short cut to internecine war. None of the putative successors to Mandela, such as Mbeki, Ramaphosa or Hani, had the authority on which unity in negotiation could be based. Only a Mandela could deliver that. Thus, the determinist might argue, Mandela and de Klerk would have been invented had they not existed.

Yet the democratic evolution of a nation is a process, usually of fits and starts. Only to the media is it a Marxist sequence of thesis, antithesis, synthesis. Even after Mandela's installation as president in May 1994, the structures of white power remained in place. The only alternative would have been anarchy. For four years the Nationalist government had progressively involved more and more ANC nominees in its decisions. By 1992, the budget and regional policy were openly negotiated with ANC shadow teams. Since 1993, the Transitional Executive Council, composed of members of both sides, had been the effective government of the country. This eased the transition and secured a bipartisan approach to policing political disturbances in Natal and elsewhere. By early 1994, the ANC was already in power if not in office.

What happened on 27 April 1994 was thus a stage along a road. It was more than symbolic but less than revolutionary. It was an event of intense political emotion. For me it transcended even the tearing down of the Iron Curtain, which I had witnessed four and a half years earlier in the countryside of Saxony. In South Africa's case I noticed that as each black minister stepped forward to take his oath, it was administered by a white official. As each subsequently announced his plans for change, white civil servants and officers sat quietly alongside. The defence force, the police, the civil service, the parastatal corporations, the edifice of white nationalism had not disappeared. It had merely been put at the disposal of black nationalism. Africanization would take a long time and nobody was in any great hurry to risk trouble by expediting it. As the Webbs said of socialism, it must respect 'the inevitability of gradualism'.

The cabinet that took office under President Mandela thus had many of the same faces as had previously sat on the Transitional Executive Council under President de Klerk. There had been a reshuffle. There were new assumptions underlying its purpose. But South Africa's government was a multiracial coalition after April 1994 as it had been before it. The constitution stipulated that it should remain so until a new constitution and new elections in 1999. This was no post-colonial revolution as seen elsewhere in Africa. There was not even a widespread changing of geographical names or defacing of statues. The best historical parallel is the 1948 handover of power by English-speaking rulers to the Afrikaner Nationalists. That too was a 'tribal' transfer. That took decades to complete.

President Mandela will have trouble aplenty keeping his coalition together and keeping his supporters in line. De Klerk has not lost his cunning, and may even take his National Party into opposition as 1999 approaches. There he may find millions of disaffected blacks, as well as the Coloureds and Asians he courted so successfully in 1994. He remains in the corridors of power. By opening them so whole-heartedly to the ANC, he ensured that the ANC kept them open to him. De Klerk, by the manner of his negotiation as much as by its content, may yet have kept hold of more power than the whites had ever dreamed possible.

On his presidential inauguration, Mandela stood in glory beneath Sir Herbert Baker's imperial Union Buildings in Pretoria. Tens of thousands of visitors, from South Africa and round the world, gathered before him and dazzled all who witnessed the scene. If he had raised his sights, however, he would have looked out over the kopjes of the Transvaal, covered with the office blocks of apartheid's white rulers and the bungalows of their white officials. If Mandela wanted a revolution in South Africa he must depend on these people to implement it. He knew that all else meant chaos. But what a dependency. After the triumph comes the beginning of the struggle, not the end. When the famous of the world had departed, I could sense Mandela whispering the cry of the revolutionary down the ages: 'My God, I was more free in prison.'

3

A LIBERAL DOSE OF
NONSENSE

No British institution is so misconstrued as the Liberal
Democrat Party. Certainly none is so indulged. Every few
months I read an article asking Whither the Liberal Democrats? Sometimes it asks Who are Liberal Democrats?
Nobody ever asks Why are the Liberal Democrats? They
have become a political constant, part of Britain's heritage,
timeless, pointless yet indestructible.

Why are they? Half a century is a long time in anyone's
politics. Yet for 50 years the Liberal Party has sought high
office in Britain and failed completely to attain it. Since the
full extension of the franchise and the rise of Labour, Liberalism has had barely a sniff of power. Dangerfield published
his *Strange Death of Liberal England* in 1935, by which time
the historical Liberal 'interest' had been taken over by the
Conservative party and the Gladstonian social conscience
taken over by Labour. The Liberal Party had been squeezed
into a small corner of the political map. No Liberal has sat
in a British cabinet since the last war. Ian Bradley's rather
desperate 1985 rewrite of Dangerfield, the *Strange Rebirth
of Liberal Britain* (the title geographically corrected), was
chiefly about how liberalism with a small 'l' had permeated
the ideas of the two big parties. He tried to maintain that

Liberals were different from Tories or Socialists in that the latter two groups would subordinate the pursuit of liberty to the pursuit of authority or equality. The trouble is that Tories and Labour supporters would disagree. The bipolarism of British parliamentary politics has concealed the extent to which the liberal consensus now dominates all parties. Parliamentary Liberalism is a club not a cause.

Yet despite their marginal status in the political spectrum and their poor showing in general elections, Liberals adorn television studios and local council chambers. They claim space and the right of reply in newspapers. Their leaders become public figures and are treated with the respect due to potential prime ministers. In any other walk of life, half a century of abject failure of an organization to achieve its central purpose would cause somebody to review that organization's *raison d'être*. No such doubt assails Liberals. They awake each morning, fresh-faced and bushy-tailed. Their last two leaders, Sir David Steel and Paddy Ashdown, have behaved as if constantly on the brink of something called a 'breakthrough'. Go out, they periodically tell their followers, and prepare for government. Yet nobody sends for men in white coats.

Under the leadership of Jo Grimond and Jeremy Thorpe, Liberals had a definable socio-sartorial status. They were represented by tweeds, corduroys and sandals, yet free of any taint of ideology, sectarianism or trade unionism. They were radical without socialism. They need have no truck with the language of priorities. Electoral impotence was a badge of honour rather than of shame. Grimond's conference speeches were proto-New Age. We Liberals, he would say with an aristocratic crescendo, believe in . . . believe in . . . well, Liberalism.

Since Neil Kinnock demythologized the Labour Party, Labour and Liberal supporters alike have found themselves wandering across a political desert blasted by Thatcherism, its new paths as yet uncharted. They bump into each other, apologize and dart off in opposite directions – only to wander in a circle and bump yet again. Labour people could at least make their way back to the oasis of socialism and the trade union, public sector interest. Liberals had no such recourse. By the start of the 1990s, *Spitting Image* could satirize the party as the 'something in between' party. The change of name from Liberal to Liberal Democrat only made fuzziness yet more fuzzy.

I thought that the departure of the sensible David Steel in 1988 might signal the final acknowledgement of defeat. The party would wind up its business, distribute its remaining ideological assets to its members and suggest to its MPs that they throw in their lot with whichever party might agree not to run candidates against them at the next election. There might be a great celebration, fireworks and essay competitions. The party of Palmerston and Gladstone might acknowledge the advent of the twentieth century and universal franchise before that century was out. To soldier on like some fissiparous Puritan sect was undignified. David Steel himself had mused in his youth that the 'emergence of a social democratic party may well come from a union of the Liberal Party and the right of the Labour Party'. Surely now that the Labour Party was indeed 'the right of the Labour Party' it was time for the union. The SDP merger was merely a first bite at the cherry. It had not achieved the breakthrough so widely vaunted ahead of the 1983 general election, despite winning just two per cent less of the total poll than Labour. If there was no way forward even in the propitious times of mid-Thatcherism, there would surely never be a better opportunity again.

But no. The Liberal Party went in quite the opposite direction. It discovered a bizarre West Country ranter whose capacity for fantasy outstripped that of all his predecessors. The Right Honourable Jeremy John Durham 'Paddy' Ashdown, former marine commando, sometime employee of Dorset county council, wine-maker and gardener, assumed the party's leadership. He braced himself under the arc lights at a party conference, narrowed his eyes and challenged the nation to take him seriously. 'Come on,' he seemed to say, 'come on, hit me. Let me show you what a gritty modern

Liberal is really made of.' A faintly theatrical sneer crossed his face. This was a different appeal from that of Grimond or Steel. I sensed the political community hesitate for a moment and wonder whether to call Ashdown's bluff. But it shrugged and said, 'All right, you win. We'll pay to watch the show one more time.'

Hitting Liberals is not easy. They do not bob or weave. They stand and absorb one punch after another, merely rolling back on their heels with a glazed look in their eyes. The media treat Mr Ashdown as a political Walter Mitty, a Screaming Lord Sutch of the shires. His dreams of power are patronized. The BBC studiously accords him and his party equal status to the two big parties. His by-election and opinion poll successes are greeted as presaging some putative general election triumph. Pollsters estimate how large a majority each success implies. Mr Ashdown is always let off lightly.

Mr Ashdown, like David Owen and David Steel, has been a disaster for the left in Britain. His desire to be all things to all voters has made him a trimmer and waffler. Mr Ashdown wants to frighten nobody and appeal to all. His slogans are vacuous. One year his watchword is 'opportunity . . . opportunity to every citizen in this land of ours'. Another year he is 'facing up to the future', a future that 'challenges each and every one of us'. Yet another has him 'putting people first and changing Britain for good'. He once told me with an earnest look that he was 'serious, workmanlike and determined to ensure that what we have we hold'. Mr Ashdown is wind without a bag, a susurration of clichés that barely turns a leaf. He has a high voter sincerity rating as a result, and guards it with ceaseless frowns, smiles and tensings of the jaw muscles.

In the 1990s, British politics has become increasingly hard to read. The collapse of deference has lead voters to treat general elections as moments to choose a prime minister, and everything else as an occasion to protest. But how to protest? How, as an elector quoted in *The Times* in May 1994 put it, to 'tell the buggers up there what we think of them?' The answer is the beaming face of Mr Ashdown. To the disaffected Tory of the Thatcher and post-Thatcher eras, the Liberal Democrats are protest without pain. They are a convenient dustbin. When Labour was in office, protest voters tended to swing to Tory. Liberals did less well under Labour. But fifteen years of Tory rule have established the Liberals as the protest party *par excellence*.

No arena of British politics stages this theatre of the absurd so well as the by-election. Time was when a by-election indicated a genuine preference between government and Opposition. Since those at Torrington and Orpington in 1958 and 1962, by-elections have offered the chance for a cry of rage against authority, the big parties and the government of the day. They are also an opportunity to register displeasure at any policy or incident, local or national, without endangering the elector's basic support for one party leader as prime minister as against another. Anything can be put in contention, a local school closure, a subsidy denied, a local character deserving of support.

Psephologists eager for polling contracts are adamant that, while by-elections are eccentric, they are eccentric in some constant manner. I find this extraordinary. There is no correlation between by-election results and general elections or even opinion poll averages. Within months of her Falklands victory, and with her popularity as high as it ever was, Margaret Thatcher lost the Tories' Birmingham Northfield constituency to Labour. Shortly afterwards she held a general election, secured an increased majority (and won Northfield back). A month after that election, a by-election was held for Lord Whitelaw's Penrith seat. His 30 per cent majority was all but wiped out by the Liberal Democrats. In 1990 the Tories lost two of their safest seats, Eastbourne and Mid-Staffordshire, defeats that played a part in the felling of Mrs Thatcher. They won both back inside two years. Tactical voting was apparently used to eject the Tory in both cases. Voters were sophisticated enough to calculate how to throw out a government MP other than at an election at which the running of the country was at stake. When it was at stake the same electors behaved quite differently.

27

Responsible pollsters have fought shy of by-elections, following a drubbing at the Brecon and Radnor by-election in July 1985. MORI's Robert Worcester reflected afterwards that so many elements are at play in a by-election that no poll can possibly come up with an accurate account of the state of play. A by-election is Liberty Hall for electors, candidates and pundits alike. Yet general election predictions are still made by national newspapers on the basis of by-election results. Mrs Thatcher's three Conservative parliaments saw 58 by-elections. Her party won just 12 of them, always with big swings against it. John Major's party had, by mid-1994, never won a single by-election. Neither prime minister had ever lost a general election. On by-election performance alone, the Liberals would have been ruling Britain for the past quarter century.

By-elections mean nothing. They are random political events, rather on the pattern of ministerial sex scandals. They are hugely enjoyable. They may be accorded political significance by the politically alert classes, but that is saying no more than that a crowd prone to panic will do so at the slightest stimulus. Any stick will do to beat a dog. If a government is in trouble, a by-election is a good enough stick. But since Liberals are the beneficiaries of that stick, every by-election 'set-back' for a government perpetuates the fantasy of a Liberal breakthrough just round the proverbial corner.

The modern Liberal Democrat Party is the creation of political Darwinianism. It has adapted itself to attract the restless dissident. It is politics without content, concern without responsibility. It is a flirtatious affair. The promiscuous Mr Ashdown relieves disgruntled Tories of having to take a deep breath and cavort with the scarlet woman of Labour. Throughout the 1980s, Labour was never able to attract sufficient anti-Tory votes to topple the government. Mrs Thatcher received some of the smallest shares of total votes given to any prime minister since the war. Labour and Liberal combined invariably gained a higher share. There was a brief moment in 1993 when Mr Ashdown's acolytes spoke of a strategic 'shift to the left'. The year before in a speech at Chard he even seemed ready to contemplate – in typically Ashdownian terms – talks about talks about pacts. This was rebuffed by Labour. Mr Ashdown declared unemployment to be the 'issue of the moment'. All enquirers were told that he was deeply concerned about it and had been so for a long time. Yet when asked if this implied a move towards the left or towards Labour, he paled with horror. No, he said, Labour was the party of the past. Did the whole world not know that there was to be a Liberal victory at the next election, or at very least at the one after that? Hope of a hung parliament springs eternal in the Liberal breast.

I sometimes wonder how long this nonsense will go on. What would it take to achieve the demise of a political party in Britain? Nobody would invent the Liberal Democrats if they did not exist. The vagaries of protest vote politics have put them in positions of some power in hung local authorities. But this power merely reflects the curiosities of local arithmetic, not some overwhelming local support for an ideology or an interest called Liberalism. The Liberal Democrats are seldom in a majority. Their power is that of the smoke-filled room, the committee bargain, the balancing vote. Nobody elects a hung council. A hung council is a political accident of which any minority party is likely to be the beneficiary. Yet local government success reinforces success at by-elections. It encourages Liberals to think they can defy half a century of history.

The political institutions of democracy are deeply conservative. In Britain they have quasi-constitutional status. From the Speaker's wig and gown to Prime Minister's Questions and points of order, the House of Commons is rooted in the past. Parliamentary time is regarded as sacred. Procedure is unreformable until occasionally it is reformed. It is the warp and woof of the constitution. The Liberal Party is part of this archaic fabric. Like the statues of great statesmen in the Central Lobby, the Liberals are part of Britain's democratic heritage. Just as Parliament keeps a niche for hereditary peers, so it keeps one for Liberals. They are the licensed third force,

Her Majesty's Loyal Dustbin for protest votes. They will live forever because nobody can think of a way of making them die.

4

YOUR VERY CIVIL
SERVANT

That very near miss for an All Souls' Fellowship
The recent compensation of a K;
The first class brains of a senior civil servant
Are sweetbreads on the road today.

JOHN BETJEMAN'S hated mandarin ended his life impaled
on the steering column of a Humber, 'where the bypass
comes out of Egham into Staines'. As he died a hundred
thousand Englishmen cheered. Why? The civil servant was
once a cherished professional, a servant of the 'civis'. The
words epitomized civility, humility and selfless duty. A certain
grandeur might be added by some exotic prefix, such as senior
or Indian or Sudanese. But the public service was more than
a dignified vocation. It carried prestige. The appellation
'Whitehall' had about it the ring of court and influence. And
since the Northcote-Trevelyan reforms of 1854, the profession could hold its head high as the epitome of merit,
selected by open examination as the only means of avoiding
'the evils of patronage'.

Here was no trace of industry, commerce or trade. Civil
servants did not get their hands dirty or associate with the
lower orders. A clerk might be a clerk but a cordon sanitaire

31

divided him from manual workers, from 'direct labour'. He
was an official. That, as Chekhov wrote, is a cog in an empire
ever so mighty. The civil servant carried in his bag the authority of kings. Small wonder that in China the mandarins
carried status second only to the emperor himself. Small
wonder that Britain's civil service gracefully accepts the title
of 'mandarinate'.

Not today. The British have become so civil-servant averse
they are ready to welcome government plans to hurl the lot
of them into the furnace of private sector competition. Plans
to this effect are before Parliament. This is seen as one privat-
ization not before its time. The Downing Street efficiency
unit – begetter of a hundred quangos, agencies and sub-
contractors – has recommended that even the most senior
Whitehall posts should be open to all applicants. A new
Northcote-Trevelyan should make not only the service open
to all talents, but each post open at each grade of seniority.
The civil servants' post-entry closed shop should end.

This is subversion at the heart of the nation state. Civil
servants are to be held 'accountable' for policy failures, or at
least for failures of implementation. Those who cannot perform will be sacked. The days, so the efficiency unit is
reported to say, of 'cloistered worlds and magic paths to the
top' are over. Ministries will be subject to death by a thousand
clichés. They must be ventilated from outside, market-tested,
no longer free to 'grow their own timber'. The new civil
service must be infused by the skills of those with 'frontline
experience in commerce and industry'. There must be no such
thing as tenure for life. A minister must have producer choice.
If he does not like an official – or at least an official's advice
– he must be able to sack him.

Clearly a decade of Whitehall abuse has reached a climax.
Antagonism to all forms of bureaucracy is universal, whether
European or BBC or town hall or health service. Cursing
bureaucrats is a national sport. There are marker bureaucrats,
second-guessing bureaucrats, market-testing bureaucrats,
regulatory bureaucrats. There are health and safety bureaucrats (who bankrupt you), VAT bureaucrats (who drive you

to suicide), hospital bureaucrats (who kill you). The education department is creating a brand new bureaucracy to run the nation's schools when they have been taken from the hands of local councils. There are bureaucrats to police the Citizen's Charter, to test how long it takes an official to answer a phone or reply to a letter. There are even bureaucrats to 'cut red tape' and reduce bureaucracy. There are 10 new government offices in the regions to act as 'one stop' local bureaucracies. The creatures are now swarming out of Whitehall to infest every home and small business, every doctor's surgery and lawyer's office. Shakespeare's revolutionary Dick the Butcher cried, 'First thing we do, let's kill all the lawyers.' Today he would kill all the pen-pushers.

So nemesis has come. From the elevated scorn of *Yes, Minister* to the columns of *Private Eye*, the proliferation of titles, deputies, functions and assistants demands expiation. Modern government has become aloof and must be made more responsive to its consumers. It must be 'reinvented in an entrepreneurial mode', in the jargon of Osborne and Gaebler's *Reinventing Government*. It must become more like the private sector. And since this is asking too much of the existing Whitehall career structure, that structure must go. The critics accuse the modern civil servant of being able to do only addition and multiplication, not division and subtraction. Closed shops have led to elephantiasis, and elephants move slowly and eat voraciously. Margaret Thatcher once told a group of railway managers, 'Of course if any of you were any good you would be not here but in private industry.' There they would really have to perform. So the efficiency unit appears to be pushing at an open door. We British are famous for our exemplary punishment. As Voltaire noted, we execute a few officers from time to time to encourage the others.

Let us calm down and take this argument apart. The first hurdle to any drive to reduce red tape is that it rarely has that effect. Bureaucratic change is bureaucratic growth. The only case of an administrative tier being cut rather than redefined was the Greater London Council and the other Metropolitan counties in the mid-1980s. They had to suffer complete abolition to yield a saving. Even then the savings proved much smaller than expected. London bureaucrats shifted to 'residuary bodies'. Others became an agency. Others still moved to the boroughs. Most GLC functions continued in being under another guise. Bureaucracy obeys some thermodynamic constant of its own. It cannot cease to exist.

The reason is partly that politicians do not have the guts to endure the backlash. Every bureaucrat fired can always show that some disaster was the result of his removal: be it a disease or a fire or a battered child or a fraudulent subcontractor. Cutting out a subcontracted service or a grant to an outside body or a new building is a more painless way to reduce costs, if costs must be reduced. Public administration is a growth industry in every country in the world. In part this is a sign of a benign society, of the desire of democracies for more orderly, more caring oversight. The public may hate civil servants but it wants more 'civil services' and wants them better run. Parliament, as proxy for the public, forces government ever further into the lives of citizens. It supervises and makes more safe their pleasures. It criminalizes their narcotics, their dogs, even the separated husbands of their children. General practitioners, farmers, teachers, builders all attest to the rise in form-filling. When government privatizes something – be it the telephones or the gas industry or the railway – it makes sure there are still civil servants to monitor and regulate.

Government in the form of politicians cannot abolish government in the form of civil servants. The two have a symbiotic relationship. The one requires the other to be itself. But the politicians need to appear to be abolishing civil servants, or at least to be fashioning them to new tasks. So ministers take Osborne and Gaebler seriously. The new 'entrepreneurial' minister need no longer sit atop an empire of clerks. He defines a public need and purchases services from the private sector to answer that need. In addition to getting a 'bigger bang for the budgeted buck', the entrepreneurial minister wants to circumvent the lobbies and the

34

short-termism of the old party politician. His environment is one of constant reform. It is one in which, say Osborne and Gaebler, 'substantive change is risky and politicians are punished far more for trying something and failing, than for running a mediocre or ineffective government.' Yet they must keep trying, for that is what the public expects of them. So they read the book and struggle to harness market disciplines to the great game of policy. Since bureaucrats know nothing of privatizing railways or denationalizing hospitals or reorganizing prisons, the private sector must supply the answer.

There is some sense in this jargon. In Britain, the bulk of the civil service is being redefined. The concept of 'general administration' is being stripped of its bluff. The administrator is being de-professionalized. He is a manager, supplying the public a service at arm's length from the central organs of government. Here in the nether reaches of social service offices or VAT inspectorates or defence bases, officials toil away, requiring only to manage and be managed more effectively. They will be expected to declare objectives and deliver against a target. Were it not for the absence of shareholders, they might as well be in a building society or travel agency. If they fail to meet their targets, they can be fired. Otherwise, they will rest in peace.

Where does this leave the first-class brains? The answer should be, no different. The civil servant should be regarded as like the doctor or lawyer or engineer, upholder of a body of knowledge and practice acquired over years of indenture. Yet the primary task of the senior civil service has nothing to do with management. Strip away management, hive it off to a thousand agencies and quangos, and there is still a crucial function at the heart of government. It is to help democratically elected politicians recast their random thoughts as implementable policy, and in the process to stop them making fools of themselves and democracy. Civil servants must be able to draw a route map through the daily storms of circumstance. They must run the country, even as others *try* to run it. They must know what is a good or bad Act of Parliament, a good or bad treaty, a good or bad regulation. Such officials are the simultaneous translators of the language of politics into the language of government.

I do not believe these tasks can be performed by people with no acquired knowledge of them, with no experience of politics or government. Such advisers require a strict independence of those in politics to whom they are proffering advice and of those outside government with whom government must deal. Their intellectual and personal integrity must be total. This to me is the definition of a profession. Countries that do not have a 'professional' corps of senior public officials, of which America is one, suffer for it. They get worse government, and certainly more costly and corrupt government. Nor are there short cuts to this integrity. Headhunters may believe they can spot it and hire it from the private sector, supplanting existing civil servants at a minister's will. But if an official does not have job security independent of his or her political boss, the integrity must be compromised.

By all means let this élite gain experience of the world beyond its corridors. Let it know the horrors of being on the receiving end of policy, broaden its horizons. But Britain, for better or worse, is governed by a club of politicians operating in the rough-house of Whitehall and Westminster. Surviving this rough-house is a specialized skill, not an easy one, nor one readily acquired. It has little in common with the skill that makes for success in business. The civil servant needs to offer a deferential steer, not an unequivocal lead. Former businessmen rarely succeed in Whitehall, any more than former civil servants succeed in business. These are distinct vocations.

Many believe, with some justice, that the quality of central government decisions declined in the 1980s and 1990s. Lady Thatcher's administration was seeking to push through a revolution and regarded most advice, including that from civil servants, as hostile. Ministers were encouraged to stand up to advice, to gainsay it, to write their own white papers and edit their own legislation. The resulting upsets were spectacular. The poll tax was introduced then abandoned, armies were cut and uncut, police were centralized and decentralized, curriculums were written and rewritten. Most if not all the faults laid at the door of government were faults of political decision, not of execution. As the draftsmen of Lady Thatcher's round dozen of local government bills protested, there was no way a really bad policy could be turned into a really good bill.

We need to reassert the virtues of the senior civil servant. The quality of British public administration derives from the tension between its permanent and its temporary elements: between the aspirations of politicians and the need for sound judgment and probity in implementation, between a good idea and what is practical. This tension requires two conditions. The permanent needs to be reasonably secure in its permanency; the temporary needs to be reasonably temporary. If the civil servant is made nervous and insecure – at risk of dismissal and uncertain of a career prospect beyond his present post – the tension snaps. The civil servant becomes a surrogate politician, always on the look-out for promotion, working not for this job but for the next.

The longevity of the 1979 Tory administration, longer than any since the last war, has eroded the institutional independence of the higher civil service. Senior officials, especially those close to No. 10 Downing Street, have come to behave like ministers. While the forms of deference are observed, the reality is of a mêlée of Cabinet Office and Downing Street officials and ministers wrestling collectively with each so-called crisis. Orders are issued from a centralized command to other minister/official teams in the field. Senior officials become associated with ministers and move round Whitehall with them. This is not the fault of officials, more the fault of the British electorate. But it has made easier the assault on civil service professionalism launched by the efficiency unit in 1993 and the subsequent 1994 white paper.

Let us privatize government services. Let us hive regulators into agencies and agencies into regulators. Let us turn embassies into trade offices and ambassadors into hotel managers. Forty per cent of the domestic product goes into government activity. Ninety per cent of public administration is pure management. There are jobs aplenty for open competition. But at the heart of government is a true profession, discrete from those of private business or public sector management. It is the profession of giving advice. Such a profession need not be a closed shop, but it must have the characteristics of a profession. It must have codes, loyalties, networks, even a certain smugness. There must be some sense of a graded career, of a hierarchy distinct from the hierarchy of politics with which it is dealing. Otherwise civil servants might as well resign and form consultancies, hiring themselves to parties and to Secretaries of State on taking office. A civil service must feel itself truly free to say the unpalatable, even at risk of being wrong.

The parliamentary system in Britain offers a sort of accountability for the mistakes of government. That accountability is crude and after the event. Policy should be tested in the fire of confidential advice, before being tested in that of parliamentary or electoral retribution. The minister is the boss. The minister has absolute power over decision. The minister must not have absolute power over advice preliminary to decision. The adviser's first loyalty must be to his or her profession, that of giving independent advice. I see the British civil service as a surrogate parliament, deliberating on ministerial policy, scrutinizing ministerial decisions before their implementation. Such a function is a vital, surviving pluralism at the centre of government. The steady expansion of political patronage in appointments to public bodies, outside the purview of my élite, has greatly increased the power of politicians. It may be that, once upon a time, civil servants were too strong in relation to ministers. That is no longer the case. The balance has tilted towards politicians. It should not tilt any more. Here is a constitutional equilibrium that should be sustained. Spread one half of it over the Staines bypass and who knows what other accidents may follow.

5

FRANKLY FRANKS

A TALL white-haired figure was striding towards us down the High in Oxford. His eyes were open but strangely unfocused. His great brow was tilted like a radar scanner towards Heaven. 'We have just seen', said my companion, 'the original pillar of the Establishment.'

We had just seen Oliver Franks. He was already a lofty enigma. Over the previous decade he had apparently declined to run successively the Treasury, Nato, the BBC, *The Times*, the Coal Board, British Railways, British Petroleum, Harrow School and, for good measure, the Bank of England. The implication of such temptations, assuming all had been offered rather than just mooted, is that Franks was the most outstanding talent not just of his generation but of almost any generation. At the time of my sighting, he had just taken a ten-fold cut in salary from his job as chairman of Lloyds Bank to return to Oxford as Provost of Worcester. This merely ensured a further elevation in his moral authority. As his path took him towards Carfax, a sea of buses seemed to part at his approach, as if by a miracle.

Whatever might or might not have been Franks's abilities, such a polymath is inconceivable today. The Treasury goes to an economist, Nato to a soldier, the railways to a railwayman and *The Times* to a journalist. No more can a 'good man' turn his hand to anything. As a result, our age suffers from an apparent dearth of good men. Gone are the Frankses, Beveridges, Redcliffe-Mauds. They were above party. I cannot imagine to whom a prime minister would turn to set up a Nato, or engineer a Marshall Plan, or forge a special relationship with America. Almost certainly he would turn to a former politician or a 'sound' acolyte. There is nobody who passes muster as philosopher, administrator, diplomat, banker and grand inquisitor, all in one. There is no Prospero to stand guardian as one-man supreme court and arbiter of the unwritten constitution. These men were backstops to democracy, able men, an aristocracy of virtue. And even if they were not really so, they were perceived as so by their contemporaries. The Establishment confidence trick held its confidence.

What was it about Franks? The answer is hard to discern. Only one biography of the man has appeared – *Founding Father* by Alex Danchev, 1993 – and that is so short as to be more of a biographical essay. Danchev's thesis is that the key to Franks was specifically his distance from anything that might pass for an Establishment. Students of this concept such as Henry Fairlie and Anthony Sampson define it as embracing people of a certain background who run the central institutions of the state. They share common assumptions and, by implication, common faults. They meet regularly at work or leisure. They give each other jobs and they 'see each other all right'.

Even on these terms, Franks did not qualify. He was an outsider in almost every context in which he found himself. He was the son of a Congregational minister from Bristol. He went from Bristol Grammar School to Queen's College, Oxford, where he studied and briefly taught philosophy. He went on to Glasgow and the University of Chicago. His wife was a Quaker from a similar background to himself and their marriage appears to have been quiet, stable and ungregarious. The Second World War released Franks from what might have become the bondage of his first career choice, as it

40

released many others of his generation. As Danchev says, he did not excel as a philosopher, any more than he excelled in the conviviality that is part of the intellectual life of an Oxford college. Despite this apparent incompatibility, he returned to Oxford after the war, left to become British ambassador to Washington but returned to it in 1952 at the age of 47. He held no further public office. Franks was member of no magic circle, no coterie, no club (apart from the Athenaeum). He was cold and forbidding. He was something distinct: a one-man reputation, non-partisan, uncorruptible, without baggage. He was the epitome of sound judgment.

Franks in other words was the antithesis of the Establishment. He entered government service as a temporary civil servant in the Ministry of Supply during the war. He brought to its purposes a cool head and an analytical mind and rose to become its Permanent Secretary when still in his thirties. This would have been inconceivable in peacetime. Towards the end of the war Franks was transferred to the Marshall Aid programme. Again his coolness under pressure, his ability to chair a meeting and keep its minutiae in his head, proved invaluable. In the uncertain atmosphere of post-war European-American diplomacy, he was able to reassure nervous Europeans and to flatter powerful Americans. He brought to each negotiation an almost mechanical brilliance, devoid of personality except such personality as was required by the matter in hand. He appeared to have no interest, no side, no hidden motive except the common good. Colleagues found his detachment eerie.

The result, says Danchev plausibly, was that Franks could take the lion's share of credit for the success of Marshall Aid and for the robustness of the subsequent Nato framework. Yet no sooner were they established than he returned to Oxford, as if fleeing the lights and the pressure to contemplate in hermetic seclusion. He was pursued and asked by the Prime Minister, Clement Attlee, to cement the new Anglo-American relationship by going to Washington as ambassador. He returned to the fray, and placed the final, crucial piece in the jigsaw of collective security, negotiating with the

Americans the terms of the nuclear guarantee that formed the backbone of the Nato alliance. Franks insisted that the guarantee – that America would use its nuclear weapons to defend Europe from any Soviet aggression – had to be made explicit. Truman had wanted the pledge to be merely a verbal understanding between leaders.

Franks knew that this was not enough. He was dealing with a vacillating and exhausted Labour government and a no less hesitant American administration, vulnerable to post-war isolationism. The nuclear guarantee had to be signed in blood, if Congress was to accept its binding character from one administration to the next. It also had to be signed in blood if insecure Europeans were to believe it, and if the even more insecure Soviets were to realize that it meant what it said. Franks, according to Danchev, was often fighting alone to press the significance of each of these components, as if bringing the skills of linguistic philosophy to bear on international relations. He had to sell the guarantee to Congress, lobbying personally on Capitol Hill. The nuclear guarantee was the central construct of four decades of peace between the world powers. Its terms were tested close to catastrophe. Yet it held, and holds still. Franks's achievement ranks with the greatest in diplomatic history.

To deconstruct Franks's career we must first accept the fact of the war. This event traumatized the careers of senior figures in every profession. It exposed weaknesses and promoted strengths. It wiped out hierarchies and tore up rule books. Both the wartime coalition and the post-war Labour government were open to all talents out of sheer necessity. By the end of the war, Franks the obscure philosophy don possessed a vital Establishment tag, he was known as 'able' in the right quarters. When Labour came to power in 1945 it was not too proud to go outside its immediate circle for appointments. Ernest Bevin, a trade unionist, had come to know Franks during the war and became his patron. Franks in turn could chat with Whitehall grandees such as Robert Hall, Frank Lee and Edwin Plowden, true Establishment men. When Attlee was asked why he had sent to Washington an ambassador with no known Labour sympathies, he replied 'because he is the best man for the job'.

Conventional sociology holds that post-war Britain was class-ridden and hidebound. The civil service, Foreign Office, ancient universities, City and professions were based on inter-locking networks of those with similar outlooks. I believe this was less true then than it is now. Certainly there was a more pluralistic respect for institutions and their leaders. Politicians would not, for instance, have considered it proper, or even constitutional, to intrude on the autonomy of judges, local councils or university governors. The Establishment was an open one. Ministers would be seen at Oxbridge high tables and rub shoulders with a cross-section of political views at clubs and country weekends. People within the patronage loop of Downing Street knew people outside it. Their concept of ability may not have embraced every walk of life. But it was wider than it is now. Few modern governments could say with Attlee's confidence that he knew who would be the 'best man' for any job. They do not know best men, only loyal ones.

Some time ago I asked a government minister how the Home Secretary would choose members for the latest round of quangos, some committees to take the police out of the hands of local councils. 'He will do what we all do,' he said. 'He will ask his secretary to get in touch with the Whips' Office and go through the usual list.' The barrel of 'sound' Tories or 'sound' businessmen would again be scraped. Some-body, anybody, would be sought from this narrow category to fill the 42,600 jobs now in the patronage of ministers. Health boards, urban development corporations, curriculum committees, central funding councils, the jobs to be filled by Downing Street compare with the patronage enjoyed by an eighteenth-century ruler. The shop may have changed its wares, but it is as 'closed' as ever. Even the committee that scrutinizes political honours is composed exclusively of party politicians.

The only fount of patronage to rival that of Downing Street is the Lord Chancellor's office. This selects not just judges but also the chairmen of the *ad hoc* tribunals and enquiries that proliferate in a country with no supreme administrative court. These jobs used to be the preserve of men such as Franks. For 30 years after his retirement from public life, he sat in waiting as a *deus ex machina* to investigate the misdemeanours of the state. He was not of the Establishment but was its hired hand. He was the mandarinate's own 007, brought in to crack the toughest cases. He was careful to accept only those that he thought he could crack. Official secrets, ministerial memoirs, the banking system and Oxford University all fell under his searching gaze. They were difficult, but since they were regarded as insoluble by anybody else they only enhanced Franks's reputation. As in diplomacy so in judiciary, says Danchev, 'a man is judged not by his brilliance but by his rectitude.'

Thus this extraordinary man saw his final apotheosis. The Thatcher government found itself in the spring of 1982 in a particular bind. It had promised an enquiry into the events leading up to the Argentinian invasion of the Falklands, but dared not go for 'one of us'. All the usual candidates to chair such an enquiry were either unavailable or likely to be partisan. I remember a cabinet official at the time explaining why no judge had been considered. Judges, he said in a significant revelation, were good at arriving at the truth, but less good at qualifying the truth with a sense of proportion. (It was a point forgotten by his successors in appointing Lord Justice Scott to head the arms-for-Iraq enquiry of 1993–4.)

Even in retirement and at the age of 77, Franks was the only veto-proof name that ministers and officials could produce. The Cabinet Secretary, Sir Robert Armstrong, took himself to Oxford to see whether Franks was up to such a job. 'Did he still have his marbles?' was the way Armstrong's mission was leaked from Downing Street. The response was positive. Franks offered Mrs Thatcher what she most needed, incontrovertible moral integrity. No he was not 'Establishment man', which might well have rendered him partisan in the quest for victims in the Falklands invasion débâcle. He had become a virtual hermit in his North Oxford house.

Nobody in the Opposition, no sceptical journalist or historian, no nervous diplomat or spy could possibly protest at the name of Franks. When he asked his calm, quiet questions, some higher voice appeared to be speaking. As one witness remarked, 'I felt that if I lied, a hand would come down from Heaven and squash me flat.' Franks's enquiry into the Falklands invasion was conducted according to his own terms of reference. It was his most difficult undertaking yet. A collection of safe privy councillors was brought together by Whitehall to support him. Nobody was in any doubt whose name would be on the final report.

Franks exonerated Margaret Thatcher and her administration but did so in terms that could be read a number of ways. To Falklands triumphalists, including Lady Thatcher, the exoneration was complete. When I spoke to Franks about this five years later, he summoned up a smile. Parts of his report did not, to my mind, vindicate the final exoneration. The reply was pure Franks. I had to recall the mood of the time, he said. Britain had won a military victory against the odds. The evidence of earlier intelligence failures and political shortcomings was in his report, to be read by those who wished to read them. 'Read the whole report,' he said to any who criticized the exoneration. If the political community wished to believe that the invasion was the fault of nobody in London, let them. If they wanted to find lessons, he offered lessons aplenty.

I think Franks let the government off the hook over the Falklands. The intelligence failings were serious, and his committee made no effort to investigate material known to be available in Argentina. It could hardly judge whether there had been a failure of intelligence without finding out what intelligence might or should have known in the first place. Franks admitted that he accepted at face value only 'material placed before us by the intelligence services'. His committee did not ask why this material was so inadequate. Nor did the committee pursue why ministers ignored throughout 1981 the constant Foreign Office warnings that the islands were dangerously unprotected. The reason was a contempt in

Downing Street for the Foreign Office in particular and for advice that cost money in general. Nowhere did Franks touch on the climate of bickering and distrust then permeating the Thatcher government's foreign policy.

Perhaps that would have been going too far. Franks never went too far. But in talking to him I sensed that he knew that he had not gone far enough. He had pulled back deliberately. Why should he be the one to rock the boat – and take the flak? He had been invited blatantly to get the proverbial Establishment off the hook, to do its dirty work, perhaps even to take the widely disliked Margaret Thatcher down a peg or two. Instead he did what he felt the nation required, and retired smiling. That was his last laugh. Franks was irreplaceable. I think he knew it and intended, as his final performance, to prove it. From now on they could murmur in their moments of agony, 'If only we had a Franks: they don't come like that any more.'

Franks's tasks are now mostly performed by professional lawyers. They are used to investigate everything from nuclear power stations to rail crashes, football disasters, security leaks and arms for Iraq. The law is the only profession other than politics and public administration of which senior politicians have direct experience. They grant it extraordinary moral integrity in what is called 'crisis resolution'. When Edward Heath used Lord Wilberforce to concede victory to the miners in 1973, his lordship appeared to sanitize, almost sanctify, the defeat. Lawyers are more dilatory and more expensive than Lord Franks. But they are institutionally independent. And they are known to at least one government department, that of the Lord Chancellor. In the bitterness that surrounded the appointment of Lord Justice Scott to head the arms-for-Iraq inquiry, the question was constantly asked, 'Who chose him? Did nobody know him?' The exception proved the rule.

I do not think that senior politicians have consciously lost faith in the capacity of academics, soldiers, businessmen, bankers or even senior civil servants to adjudicate on the accidents of government. Those who patrol the corridors of Westminster and Whitehall no longer have time to know a wide range of people in whom to place their confidence. Pressure of work thus becomes a real constraint on effectiveness of government. The notorious Downing Street question in the 1980s, 'Is he one of us?', was as much a longing for a short cut to a quick appointment as an ideological requirement. The use of headhunters to fill Whitehall positions reflects the same paucity of acquaintanceship. In my experience headhunters rarely comprehend the networking and personal contacts important for effective public administration.

There are always Establishments running governments. The tensions and insecurities of high office find their antidote in shared backgrounds and close friendships. Continuity and speed of decision require that the people who must deal with each other must also know and trust each other. What is important is that they know and trust the widest possible circle. A competent Establishment is extrovert. It needs to know where the Oliver Frankses are hidden. I believe today's Establishment does not. It cries, ' Where is the Franks of today?' He is teaching philosophy somewhere, and nobody has heard of him.

6

THE MOST UNPOPULAR
MAN IN HISTORY

PRIME MINISTERS rank with estate agents, journalists and insurance salesmen in public distrust. The current British prime minister is John Major. As boxers are greeted on public appearance with 'the greatest of all time' so Mr Major is greeted with 'the most unpopular party leader of all time'. His unpopularity has pollsters in awe. It fills constituency back rooms with gloom. Even when his government is in good shape, when the economy is improving and Mr Major wins battles at home and abroad, he remains more unpopular than ever. His press notices are as awful as Chamberlain's. He ranks with George IV, Richard III, even Ivan the Terrible. Surely the man cannot look at his face in the shaving mirror each morning without bursting into tears. He must 'sit upon the ground/ And tell sad stories of the death of kings/ How some have been depos'd, some slain in war,/ Some haunted by the ghosts they have depos'd.'

Prime ministerial unpopularity has become Churchill's riddle wrapped in an enigma. It does not look right. Opinion polls since Mr Major's apparently counter-cyclical 1992 election victory have shown less than 20 per cent of the nation 'approving' of his performance. Even the eccentric Liberal Democrat leader, Paddy Ashdown, was regarded as likely to make 'a better prime minister'. Mr Major's Conservative Party was also at a historic low in the polls and lost every by-election, local election or European election that came its way. He was bottom in almost every character rating, such as good in a crisis, capable leader, or trustworthy. The only consolation was that he was not alone. Every democratic leader was in a similar predicament, not least the present and past American presidents. Even Lady Thatcher, much lauded after her going as a strong populist, was regularly more unpopular as prime minister than any of her predecessors.

I fear we are at the mercy of our old friend, statistics. Polling figures suggest that leadership popularity is a strange indicator. It gyrates wildly and has done so for all prime ministers since this polling began after the last war. Macmillan's approval rating varied from 54 per cent (1957) to 35 per cent (1958), Wilson's from 69 per cent (1966) to 27 per cent (1968) and back to 57 per cent (1975). Lady Thatcher scored an unprecedentedly low 25 per cent in 1981. She was at 50 per cent two years later, well after the Falklands War, but fell to 36 per cent soon afterwards. John Major was high at first, fell back, rose again with his 1992 election victory, then plummeted below the previous lowest point. As Robert Worcester of MORI put it, Mr Major's picture was changing faster than that of Dorian Gray.

Like crime figures, polling statistics have about them a specificity that is irresistible to press, politicians and public alike. A figure is a fact. It is difficult to gainsay and few know how to do so. Pundits are still locked in the certainties of the Old Mathematics, where probability, risk theory, grey areas and fuzzy logic are as yet untaught. Numbers 'must be true'. Yet what could be less quantifiable than our 'approval' of somebody we do not know yet whose name and image represent so much that affects our daily life? We are here dealing not with an economic aggregate or a fact of science but with the public's use of a word to describe a mood. The scope for that mood to feed on statistics about itself must be considerable. Not surprisingly, mood cycles tend to be more mercurial than any others in politics.

The press feeds on this. A politician who is down can be kicked further down. Indeed, when better to kick him, asked Iain Macleod. Newspapers are idle killers. They sniff the air. They see a buck gone lame and single it out from the herd. It is 'only a matter of time' before he goes. He will be gone by Christmas, by Easter, by summer. There need be no more substance to this hunt than a temporary attack of political jitters. Yet it feeds into the approval rating. Mr Major's unpopularity did not reflect any deep ideological division in his cabinet. Indeed his cabinets have been loyal and admiring of his performance – in stark contrast to Lady Thatcher's. No cabinet colleagues were overwhelmingly more popular than he was. Certainly he was no rough and tough leader, but that was why he was selected. He and his colleagues were exhausted with Lady Thatcher's style of rule.

There is truth perhaps in the saying that the British Establishment likes to be ruled if not by an aristocrat then by a thug, if not by heredity then by muscle. It likes to know where it stands with its leader. I doubt if the British people take the same view. Lady Thatcher and Winston Churchill, both seen as strong leaders, were neither of them specially popular. For popularity we must look at the milder characters of Macmillan, Wilson and Callaghan. Macmillan's approval rating tumbled after his notorious night of the long knives, when he sacked half his cabinet. Even so, most prime ministers score five to ten points above their party in the approval stakes. Not Mr Major. In 1993–94 he ran behind even the benighted Conservative Party.

We might dismiss all this as mere poll babble. The polls are known to get things wrong on occasions. Why should they not be at sea on a topic as ephemeral as the 'approval' of a political leader? They may say they are recording the answers to a fixed question over time, but who can tell how people's understanding of questions may change? And the answers appear ever more paradoxical. In a Gallup survey in mid-1993, Mr Major's approval rating was at an all-time low. Yet when the same sample was asked if he should therefore resign and give way to some other leader, 51 per cent said he should stay, including 78 per cent of Tories. And when the same sample was asked who would win the next election, 41 per cent of them said the Tories and only 34 per cent said Labour. Yet the group said that 'in an election tomorrow' it would vote 44 to 23 per cent in favour of Labour. Something odd must be going through the electorate's mind when confronted by the pollster.

My answer may find little favour with conventional psephology. Political scientists accept that modern British voters are throwing away the old clothes of family, geography or class identity with a particular party. Party deference is waning. We know from the decline in membership and attendance at party meetings that electors are losing interest in conventional institutions. They remain 'political'. They flock to conservation groups, neighbourhood watch schemes, planning enquiries. They are avid joiners of clubs and associations. Every interest group, from bird lovers to ramblers to motorway opponents, has its adherents. Many of these can be politically active as lobbyists. But they have little to do with loyalty to party. Parties are unfashionable things. Membership is not readily admitted. Each year on the doorstep fewer voters recite the phrase, 'Oh, we are Labour (or Conservative) here'.

When asked their political allegiance directly, either by a pollster or in a polling booth, voters don one of two sets of new clothes according to the occasion. One is worn once every four or five years to a general election and is smart and solemn. Such elections are not hypothetical. They matter. Even if the outcome in a particular seat is a foregone conclusion, the elector declares his or her faith in the process and his decision on who is best to enter Downing Street. There is some evidence that tactical voting at general elections is increasing. But it is still a small phenomenon. Eighty per cent of voters revert to a former party loyalty at general elections. It may be no more than one cross in 30 million. But to each democrat this vote is the sacred moment.

I believe voters remove this set of clothes as soon as they leave the polling booth. They then put on a quite different set, chosen more casually, when invited to give their views on the government of the day. The answer is likely to be negative. Democratic electors do not like governments, and like them less and less. They may express this dislike to pollsters and returning officers as a 'don't know', or an abstention, or a Liberal Democrat protest vote, or even a gesture to the Greens, as in the 1989 European election. The form of question is largely immaterial. From the pollster it may be specific: how would you vote in an election held tomorrow? Since there is to be no election 'tomorrow', the respondent behaves like a shrewd minister on television. He answers a slightly different question: how are you feeling towards the government just now? The political event to which he is contributing is not an election but a headline in tomorrow's newspaper.

Such incidents offer us fleeting moments on the political stage, like appearing in a television audience. To the pollster, the respondent may be solemnly pondering whom he would like to see in office. The respondent does not see it thus. He treats the question quite differently, as an invitation to participate in current politics, cost-free. He can rubbish John Major without actually toppling him. This has no bearing on who sits in Downing Street but sends whoever is there an urgent message, usually of dissent. Local and by-elections are little different. Such is the diminished status of local democracy in Britain that most voters treat them like an opinion poll. (Yet where a council has established a vigorous identity, for instance by cutting local taxes as in Wandsworth or Westminster in London, voting patterns are markedly different from the national average.) By-elections offer a different opportunity. Here the required message has to be delivered by voting out the Government candidate. This may demand a sophisticated judgment about which opposition candidate is best placed to give the bloody nose. Governments almost never win by-elections. Here tactical voting is now rife. Lady Thatcher and Mr Major lost them persistently even when they were winning general elections.

After the pollsters miscalculated the outcome of the 1992

election, there was much talk of whether respondents had lied to them about voting intention, or whether there was some 'late swing' to the Tories immediately before polling day. My answer is that they do lie, but that the lie is not intentional. In the presence of a pollster, the elector is simply in message mode, not choosing mode. He wishes to convey disgruntlement, disapproval, disappointment, anger. This seldom involves a shift right across the political spectrum to the Opposition, more likely a shift to a centre party. It has no necessary connection with how that elector might behave in choosing mode. It is merely a code for a better NHS, lower interest rates or no motorway through his back garden.

To take a general election reading from such responses may once have had meaning. It does not seem to have any now. This may help explain why Governments do so badly in polls and local and by-elections up to and soon after a general election – and in 1992 even through one. There is some convergence of poll findings and general election results round the time of an actual election. I cannot believe this has much to do with Government or Opposition performance, any more than that there is a true 'mid-term' slump in party fortunes. I suspect that as an election approaches, voters are slightly more inclined to give an honest answer to the hypo-thetical question than at other times. Message mode does give way, up to a point, to choosing mode. The same goes for prime ministerial approval ratings.

Any prime minister would be foolish to ignore the messages given him by pollsters and by lesser ballots. They are sent sincerely. They may be sent in anger; they may be sent by supporters as a gentle warning or even out of kindly concern. The child that fights and screams against the parent does not necessarily want to desert home. The pupil that rebels against the teacher does not want to give up education. Democracy is wretchedly imperfect as a political carrier pigeon, especially a democracy as unpluralistic as Britain's. Across the land are millions of people mouthing into a cosmic scrambler. All that comes back is an approval rating, a satisfaction level, a protest vote. The people cannot tell the prime minister what they really think. They can only declare that they find him the 'most unpopular since records began' in the hope that he hears some cry of pain.

As for that 'general election tomorrow', what general election?

7

TRIAL BY ORDEAL

I AM told that nothing, absolutely nothing, in politics is as awful as being assaulted by the media. The reason for the assault is immaterial. It may be a public gaffe or a sexual misdemeanour or a family misfortune or even a decision to run for the party leadership. The impact is the same. The politician is not necessarily news, he is something far worse. He is the raw material for news. This concept is devoid of proportion or shading. To the reporters or cameramen on the spot, raw material is simply their candidate for a place on the front page. They do not know how big the story will play. Editors will determine later how newsworthy the victim's fate may or may not be by nightfall. For the time being he is on death row, readied for execution irrespective of reprieve.

Telephoto lenses are turned on the great man's home by day and night. His footsteps are dogged at work. When he appears in public, embarrassing questions are screamed at him in the hopes of catching a foolish answer. The slightest slip is transmitted instantly to a waiting world. Reporters are told to telephone spouses with libellous questions and innuendos. Relatives are pestered: 'I'm awfully sorry to bother you, but are you aware that your son-in-law is

55

allegedly . . .' Every past scandal and error of judgment, financial, professional, matrimonial, is dredged from the cuttings and plastered on the wall for public notice.

Where the topic is a politician's sexual life, the media invent ludicrous 'public interest' defences for their prurience. David Mellor, at the time of his fall, was described as 'too tired' to prepare his ministerial speeches. Lord Parkinson's mind was reputedly 'not on his job' shortly before his first resignation. The harassment of families is inhuman. Wives and children, the bereaved and the grief-stricken are not spared. In no other walk of life is the punishment so disproportionate to the putative crime. Trial by ordeal was supposedly abolished by Innocent III. It is with us still.

Trial by ordeal has a more respectable pedigree than is normally credited. In the twelfth century such antique tests of innocence as trial by armed combat were felt to be hopelessly primitive. They were replaced by such trials as retrieving a ring from a boiling cauldron, walking on five hot plough-shares, holding a searing iron ball or being immersed in a tank of cold water. Then in 1215 the Catholic Church took the view that divine intervention should not be invoked to settle personal disputes. Penal reformers called an end to such possibly blasphemous invoking of the Almighty to settle judicial disputes. It was considered barbaric. Torture was introduced instead. It was high tech, thirteenth-century and thus sophisticated.

Conservatives at the time were appalled. They recalled the great days, from Athelstan to Henry II, when Britons were 'trustworthy men of good repute, who had never failed in oath or ordeal'. If a man denied a crime and called on God as his witness, 'let him carry the hot iron'. It was, as they doubtless said, good enough for our forefathers, so it is good enough for us. Trial by ordeal was an act not just of personal but of communal absolution. Those denying crimes not easily susceptible of proof by witnesses, such as adultery, sodomy, heresy or nocturnal homicide had to be judged somehow. Ordeal was a primitive lie-detector test. You swear that you are innocent? Then carry a flaming ball for three paces, bind up your hand and if it begins to heal in three days we shall treat you as innocent. Or you may opt for being plunged into a pit of cold water to see if your body sinks like an honest person's should, or is buoyed up by air supplied by the Devil. A rope was attached to the victim to prevent drowning. This ordeal was retained for witches well into the seventeenth century: they would be condemned for 'swimming'.

Most of us would ridicule this irrational route to justice. Anthropologists are more forgiving. The ordeal, which was a feature of European justice for some four centuries, was an advance on mob rule and on the brutality of trial by challenge and usually death from sword wounds. Trial by ordeal was orderly. Judgment rested with the church authorities. It secured communal consent for a possibly fine decision. Ordeal by fire was especially useful. It required that a verdict be held over for a number of days, during which communal hysteria could calm down. The rush to judgment was postponed while the arbiter, usually a priest, decided whether wounds had healed or not. Great excitement surrounded the removal of the bandages, but the outcome was treated as final. The crime was proved or absolved on the decision of the arbiter (often after secret examination).

Robert Bartlett points out in his study of *Trial by Fire and Water* that this was not seen as especially cruel in what was anyway a violent world. It was normally voluntary and roughly half its victims were, according to available records, judged to be innocent. A calloused medieval hand or foot was not as delicate as one of ours today. Much appears to have depended on the manner in which innocence was first protested and the decorum with which the ordeal was endured. Tristan's Isolde was acquitted of adultery after trial by ordeal even when guilty (in the legend, not the opera). Adam Smith approved of the fact that ordeal at least 'put a speedy end to a dispute'. The medieval historian, Peter Brown, is similarly sympathetic about this form of justice: 'There was a built in flexibility . . . that enabled the group to maintain a degree of initiative quite contrary to the explicit ideology of the ordeal.' Church and state law systematized ordeal, before finally banning it. Trial by torture which supplanted it was crude and cruel by comparison. Apart from its other obvious defects, it was administered by the prosecution.

I believe we have come full circle. A modern democracy has revived trial by ordeal as a way of testing fitness to govern. The physical agony may no longer be applied, but the psychological agony is every bit as intense. Trial by media is savage and primitive. Those who enter politics must accept that they may at any time have to submit to ordeal by camera and notebook, videotape and soundbite. They must prove their innocence, sometimes of the most trivial or personal offences, or be judged guilty.

The most fearsome medieval test was by the 'triple ordeal'. This involved a sequence of trials, including carrying a hot ball weighing three times the normal weight. Modern politics has a similar sequence. It runs as follows. First a tabloid newspaper reveals some detail of a politician's private life in lurid and usually part fabricated detail. This publicly humiliates the individual and his family. Three days later, the world holds its breath. Has the scorched flesh healed or has it turned to pus and gangrene? After a week the quality press discusses *ad nauseam* whether the tabloid revelation, true or false, has rendered the victim a 'political liability'. This becomes the gossip of the corridors and lobbies. At this point, the victim is watched even more intently. Does he sink like an honest man or does he struggle to stay on the surface? Then comes the third trial, the 'ordeal of the blessed morsel'. (This used to involve the victim being given a mouthful to see if he swallowed cleanly or choked on his sins.) The Whips' Office waits to see if the excuses come straight, if the 'constituency is behind him', or whether the MP panics and gasps whenever questioned in public.

Of all this Downing Street is the arbiter, but with a wary eye to the mob. The prime minister and his advisers watch to see how the wounds heal, how the mob reacts to the sizzling flesh or the arms threshing in water. He must decide what impact a decision either way may have on his own position, on his reputation for toughness or compassion. An agonizing wait ensues. Will resignation be invited, or does the telephone stay silent?

I conclude that the concept of the ordeal has an archaic legitimacy. Ordeal by media reflects Britain's political frustration. The country lacks the constitutional checks enjoyed by countries abroad. American electors can judge their president and impede his actions at Congressional elections every two years. In Britain we can do this only every five years. Bad government cannot be defeated in the Commons or on the field of battle. Government is impregnable to everything but its own mistakes. Thus disenfranchized for a term, electors seek redress. If they cannot seize ministers by the scruffs of their necks they can at least seize them by their vitals. When ministers scream and fall, the public can declare that Fate has spoken, that justice is done, an example has been set.

I cannot think of any politician regarded as having been *unjustly* driven from office. Each fall from grace is seen as vindicating some virtue in media scrutiny. In a democracy public opinion is always right. A political liability is a liability. The media are the modern Furies. The Greeks knew and respected them. The Furies slept when Orestes visited Delphi. But they rose in a rage when he went to Pallas Athene and asked for acquittal on the charge of matricide. They pursued and persecuted him. They stood against him at his final trial and, when he was indeed acquitted, they were appeased only by being granted an honoured place in Athens life. The Furies were thus integral to Athenian politics and, as the chorus, to Athenian drama.

The Greek word for Furies was Eumenides, the Kindly Ones. Just so. Perhaps we should see the media in the same light. Sometimes the old ways are the best.

8

VIVA SUZMAN

Two QUALITIES I admire in a politician are anger and humour. Neither can triumph without the other. Together they do not make a completely virtuous ruler. But when a politician can sustain both for a quarter of a century against a cruel regime, that politician must be remarkable. Helen Suzman is remarkable.

I last met Mrs Suzman on 27 April 1994. That day was the climax of everything for which she had fought, a real general election in South Africa. I had asked to accompany her on a tour of inspection of polling stations in Soweto. She assured me I would find it 'terribly dull'. I did not. For her it was a royal progress. She was the champion of black freedom, the woman who had befriended political prisoners, fought for their civil and political rights, badgered and complained and made a nuisance of herself through 36 lonely years in the South African parliament. She was 76 and retired except for her membership of the Independent Electoral Commission (IEC). Now she was going to meet the people of Soweto at the moment of their, and her, triumph. She would share that victory with them in joy.

'Mama Suzman,' they cried as we arrived at each station. 'Viva Suzman . . . We know you . . . You are so young! Why can we not vote for you?' The queues stretched for miles across Soweto and Mrs Suzman was appalled by them. To a South African white person, they were an offence. To a member of the IEC they were a sign of incompetence, a manifestation of poor quality service. Yet to the people of Soweto, a queue was part of daily life. These queues were also special. They were holy. As the day wore on I watched them snaking across the hillsides and through the dusty streets of Soweto. They were mesmeric, as if sanctified by their purpose. These people were not angry. They were not particularly jolly. The atmosphere was that of pilgrims, quiet, dignified, sure of purpose. The waiting time might be four hours, but the four hours was the consummation of half a century of journeying. On that day, Soweto might have been medieval Vézelay or Santiago.

The arrival in their midst of this stubborn, determined lady seemed the final benefaction on their liberty. She could have claimed a place on any party's election list. 'Come here Helen and tell us who to vote for,' they shouted. She protested that she had done with politicking. But old habits die hard. She took her responsibility as an IEC member seriously. Her biting tongue, for so long the lash of apartheid ministers, had lost none of its sting. 'How long have you been waiting?' she demanded of a star-struck old lady in Dube, quite overwhelmed at shaking the hand of the great person. 'Oh Mrs Suzman, no trouble. Four hours but that's fine. I've been waiting 46 years and I'm very happy.' The Commissioner brushed aside such sentiment. 'Nonsense, not good enough. Four hours. Disgraceful. Where's the returning officer? What's happening. No ballot boxes left! Phone the headquarters immediately.'

To Helen Suzman, making blacks wait all day in the hot sun to vote was a slap in the face from the old regime. Yet she could not blame the old regime. The cause of the inefficiency in Johannesburg was mostly black administrators nominated by the African National Congress. This was the new regime and it augured ill for the future. At the time, we did not even know how long the solemn quiescence of the crowds would last. Every time doors were closed because boxes were stuffed full or because returning officers ran out of stamps or pencils, a restive murmur would surge back along the queue. In the past, Soweto had not forgiven those in authority who made mistakes. Would it show tolerance when the mistakes were in a good cause? Soweto tends to smell a trick first and ask questions later.

In an Orlando primary school we encountered Mrs Tutu, wife of the archbishop and a prominent ANC supporter. Her partisan credentials had not stopped her from becoming the local returning officer. Hers was one of the more efficient stations. Her waiting time was down to one hour. Helen and she embraced with cries of delight and then settled down to berating the incompetence of all authority, as if oblivious of the fact that authority now rested with them. At Dube's White Church polling station a harassed official, immaculate in his best suit, did not know whether to regale his visitor with his successes or complain of his failings. He certainly deserved a Hansard Society medal for electoral improvization. With no identity stamps to hand, he had his staff tear up toilet paper and soak piles of it in invisible ink. Voters had to plunge their fists into the pile before voting. Meanwhile I saw Helen across the crowded room hurling complaints down the phone. She might have been standing in the foyer of Pretoria jail in the old days, reviling some hapless minister who never had the courage to refuse telephone calls made under the discipline of parliamentary privilege.

On we drove through the day. At one point a security car caught up with us, only to be furiously chased away. 'I have never had security and I don't want it in Soweto,' shouted Mrs Suzman. Other hangers-on came and went, an American camera crew, a reporter from the local newspaper, an enterprising American student rubbernecking on history. Somehow she outpaced them all. She was like a commander touring the front at the height of battle and finding the troops still without boots or ammunition. Every good politician knows that boxes, seals, ink and stamps are not the mere detritus of an election. They are its essence. They are the point of contact between the voter and the system. For the want of a seal a box is lost. For the want of a box a return is contested. For the want of a return a province goes and a grievance is left simmering. 'God help this country,' cried Mrs Suzman over and again. I tried to console her with the majesty of the occasion. 'Look at that queue,' she would reply. 'God help this country.'

Mrs Suzman was not just an idealist. She was a master technician of democracy. She had survived as MP for Johannesburg's wealthy Houghton constituency for 36 years by being a thorough constituency member. The Nationalist Party could taunt her, harass her, ostracize her but it could not deny her her seat, white-voted as it was. She owed her presence as a cuckoo in the apartheid parliamentary nest – for 13 years she was a one-woman party in parliament – to the voters of north Johannesburg. But while she kept up a relentless assault on apartheid, she was a conservative at heart. As her memoirs make clear, she believed in the rights of the black population and in their good-heartedness. That faith did not extend to their executive competence, any more than she had faith in the competence of the Afrikaner government. She was a free-marketeer and no friend of socialism.

I first met Mrs Suzman in 1979 in her house in Johannesburg. She shocked me by telling racist jokes about Afrikaners. I had spent much of my day hearing Afrikaners tell racist jokes about blacks, but soon learnt that gallows humour was a frequent emotional release in apartheid South Africa. She used it remorselessly in politics. She once told the Prime Minister, John Vorster, in parliament that he should visit a black township one day, but he should go 'heavily disguised as a human being'. From a man such abuse would have led to fisticuffs. From this fiesty woman it could just raise a smile.

Many years later I attended a lunch given in London by the British Foreign Secretary for Nelson Mandela, shortly after the latter's release from prison. He was seated next to Douglas Hurd and looked exhausted. As he sank into his chair his face brightened to see Mrs Suzman, an old friend, placed directly opposite him. 'Nelson,' she launched straight in. 'You are being very naughty about sanctions' – to which she was strongly opposed – 'you know you are.' Mandela smiled nervously at the company, all of whom apart from Mrs Suzman were British. He replied defensively . . . difficult issue . . . American pressure . . . arguments on both sides. She cut him short. 'Nelson, you know perfectly well . . .' and she was off. A diplomatic lunch had become a Cape Town political barbecue. Mandela relaxed. We listened as two South Africans argued their country's future, as South Africans had argued it for decades, over a plate of food. I felt we should have tiptoed away and left them to it. This was their future not ours.

Mrs Suzman lived most of her political life almost without allies. To her right were the battlements of Afrikaner Nationalism, brutal, sexist, anti-Semitic, engaged in the shambolic construction of one of the world's most unpleasant and bureaucratic regimes. She had to confront the repulsive trio of Verwoerd, Vorster and P. W. Botha. She loathed them and they her. 'If my wife chattered like the honourable lady,' said an exasperated Botha on one occasion, 'I would know what to do with her.' They muttered and sniggered during her speeches. 'Neo-communist, sickly humanist, go back to Israel, vicious little cat' were among the epithets recorded in her memoirs. Nationalist MPs seemed to like their women large and docile. They could not cope with this cheeky terrier of a female. She confirmed their worst suspicions of the English-speaking mercantilists of Johannesburg's northern suburbs. They were unsound not just on race but on gender too.

Yet Mrs Suzman won almost equal opprobrium from the left. The heavy mob of foreign liberalism accused her of 'going along with apartheid' by remaining an MP in an all-white parliament. To them she was the toy of the English rich, of 'silk stocking' Houghton. Her constituents could make money out of the sweat of the blacks then salve their consciences by putting Mrs Suzman into parliament. She served as a propaganda tool for the Nationalists. She was 'exhibit A for democracy' in a land that did not have any real democracy. She was a fraud. 'I can stand cold hate; I can't stand paternal liberalism,' said the black American politician Andy Young in an attack on her work. She cracked back, 'Oh I can be just as nasty to blacks as to whites.' In his case she proved it. I doubt if the hundreds of black prisoners whose afflictions she relieved over the years would have sided with Mr Young.

Mrs Suzman could make Margaret Thatcher seem like a shrinking violet. She spent a lifetime on democracy's wildest frontier. For four decades she gazed over the precipice at some of man's worse inhumanity to man, for 13 of them without any other supporter in parliament. She neither flinched nor turned away, only standing down when she could see her cause was won. True, her background was comfortable and her supporters rich (including Harry Oppenheimer and his Anglo-American Corporation). She had the backing of an often courageous English-language press. But there were plenty of whites who were ready to ignore the horrors on their doorstep, or consider them 'the price to pay' for prosperity and security.

Her chosen witness was perhaps an archaic one – membership of a tribally exclusive parliament – but she was living and operating under an archaic constitution. She used its own institutions as tools to attack it and relieve injustice to individuals. To South Africans who chose to live under apartheid, this was surely the one honourable course. The reason why so many whites respected Mrs Suzman – why few South Africans thought she was wrong to stand for parliament – was that they knew she was right. She was not passing by on the other side. She carried their consciences on her shoulders for all those years.

The task Mrs Suzman set herself was relentlessly to oppose the laws that apartheid placed on the statute book. The apartheid policy was never totalitarian. It was not imposed by presidential or military edict. Apartheid was the product of meticulous acts of parliament, debated on the floor of the assembly: the Mixed Marriages Act, the Terrorism Act, the Ninety-Day Detention Act, the Sabotage Act, a string of land acts stripping blacks of the right of settlement on their own property. She entered parliament at the age of 35 in 1953 and watched the dire edifice pass into law, one brick on another. She tore at the cement and occasionally punched a hole. She was no orator and no political philosopher. She was just a workaholic for justice.

The battle was a tribute to two much-abused relics of British rule on the tip of Africa, the Westminster parliamentary rule book and a mostly free press. Mrs Suzman exploited both. She exploited the right of parliamentary privilege, questions to ministers, points of order, access to government departments and institutions. She exploited the press and the journalist's natural delight in a scrap, a lone fighter, an incident, a sense of humour. De Tocqueville declared that prisons were the 'mirror and measure' of any government. Mrs Suzman was the first MP onto Robben Island and demanded and secured at Mandela's request the removal of a notoriously sadistic warder. She put down an average of 200 parliamentary questions a year. When ministers protested that this avalanche of exposure 'embarrasses us abroad' she shouted, 'It's not my questions that embarrass, it's your answers!' She was unable to stop apartheid, but she unquestionably softened its lash.

The key to Helen Suzman's success, and her staying power, was her ability to keep events in proportion, to realize that obeying some rules enabled a shrewd political tactician to bend other rules to advantage. Even when faced with the implacable horrors of Verwoerdism, she always deferred to decisions of the Speaker. She was able to read out Mandela's famous defence speech under cloak of privilege and thus ensure its media dissemination. She was never banned, nor even deprived of her parliamentary seniority. By respecting the House she secured at least grudging respect from some of her opponents within it.

A wise politician acknowledges shades of grey in an enemy. While Mrs Suzman detested men such as Vorster and his vicious police minister, Jimmy Kruger, she could like or at least sympathize with the latter's successor, Louis de Grange.

She openly admired F. W. de Klerk and he came to admire her. Yet she could hate with a public fury. Warned by a minister to 'be more careful in choosing your friends' she whipped back, 'No, only in choosing my enemies!' When an odious MP complained of the murder rate in his constituency, she told him that he should beware of ever actually visiting the place, 'or the murder rate will rise by one'. She was delighted when at the recent election the National Party published an advertisement in which it claimed to have done 'in four years what Helen Suzman couldn't accomplish in 36: you need more than a loud voice.' She was quoted as remarking, 'Really! I mean there I was, little me, against all those men all those years in parliament, and now they say that. How funny!'

I believe that the lingering traces of open politics and free speech in South Africa played a greater part in the eventual collapse of apartheid – and in the manner of its collapse – than did either its internal contradictions or any external pressure. Mrs Suzman's campaign against economic sanctions, which damaged few white South Africans but many blacks, was evidence of her courage. It imperilled her image as a liberal and probably cost her the Nobel peace prize which went to Desmond Tutu. But she believed she was right, that sanctions were immoral and counterproductive, and that was that.

Helen Suzman quotes an old African saying, 'Never argue with the crocodile when you are still in the same water.' She did. She taunted the beast from morning to night. She never took liberalism's easy cop-out, the path of ostracism, sanctions, disengagement, amnesia. She never disengaged from anything. When intolerant audiences in Europe and America abused her as racist, she bellowed back in her soft South African lilt, 'Get lost the lot of you!' South Africa could find its own salvation without them. It would and in April 1994 it did.

Democracy needs such tonics from time to time. It has too few. That day in Johannesburg ended back at Mrs Suzman's office. She was exhausted from the struggle, still fuming. She was, she admitted, 'really not cut out to be in charge of something, to support governments. I am supposed to be in opposition. I am best that way.' Soweto had seen Mrs Suzman at her best, even if this time she was opposing her own electoral organization. She appreciated the irony. Soweto proceeded to victory and Mrs Suzman to bed.

Into Society

9

GOING SCIENCE CRAZY

WAS EVER a victory so unsung? One of the great ventures in post-war economic planning was the attempt by the 1979 Tory government to produce more British scientists. The bid was based on no research, on no deep insight into the future needs of a post-industrial labour force. It was an act of faith, an *a priori* assumption. Somebody, nobody knows quite who, said that Britain 'needed more scientists'. The government obliged. But the nation said no, or at least the part of the nation that mattered. The nation won, but who dares admit it?

The consequence of this edict was to upheave the education service to a degree scarcely noticed by the public. It was the educational equivalent of a D-Day mobilization. Universities were told to deliver the goods. Whitehall brought in a grant system of which Draco would have been proud, to impose central planning on the universities. The school curriculum was torn up and teachers told what to teach, in detail running to over 300 pages of statutory instructions. Science and maths were elevated to the status of 'core' subjects, a lofty eminence shared only with English. The rest of the curriculum had to be built round them. Disobedience to this curriculum, teachers were told, would be actionable in the courts. They had to produce tens of thousands more science pupils. Comrade Stakhanov must have leapt joyous from his grave.

What happened? By the early 1990s the policy had been in force for half a decade. It failed. 1993 was the first year in which a complete cohort of pupils would have passed through the secondary school system under the new dispensation. The GCSE and A-level results for that year showed that the nation's pupils had simply turned their backs on the policy. Over its duration the number taking science GCSE had fallen by 10 per cent. In the same year entries in physics, chemistry and biology fell by 16, 14 and 12 per cent respectively. At A-level the statistics were no less disastrous for the science lobby. Physics numbers fell by 10 per cent. A-level maths was down. The rising stars were English, art, design, computing and social sciences.

Pupils clearly do not want to study science. They dislike the subject and see it as unhelpful in their careers and in later life. Questioned by researchers and the media, they announce with an impressive absence of political correctness that they find science boring. Science jobs pay badly. Students prefer the arts and social sciences. They regard them as more relevant to the world of work and play. They are more fun at university and they deliver better results in the market. Students, in a nutshell, are not to be conned or fooled.

Once upon a time the universities would have responded to this shift in consumer demand by cutting back on science courses and supplying more arts ones. Science is anyway most costly at university: laboratories are expensive and equipment needs constant updating. Arts courses are comparatively cheap. The chief cost is in housing students away from home, a long standing British extravagance. Before the new policy was ordained, universities were relatively autonomous in deciding what subjects to offer. In the great expansion of the 1960s, universities competed for students by offering the brightest applicants the best of what they wanted. True, the government paid. But the government kept its hands off what happened to the money. Only in the field of medicine did it lay down firm targets of the number of doctors it wished to see produced (with predictably disastrous fluctuations in supply and demand). Even Labour governments did not risk extending such *dirigisme*.

The present government responded to student demand by trying to stifle supply. In 1992 it cut the subsidy paid to universities for arts places by £550. A university gets just £1,300 for an arts place and £2,700 for a science one. The result was a predictable shortage of arts places and an excess of science ones. In 1993, A and B grades at A-level were needed for an arts place while E-grades would do for science. Thousands of students with A-level grades too low for an arts place had to ponder a transitional course to get a science qualification and go on to do a science degree instead, whether or not this was their preferred career.

The taxpayer was thus asked to pay out huge sums to induce poorly qualified students into a costly course that they did not want to take. Thousands of reluctant science graduates were in production, and to no purpose. The science-first policy was a manpower planning version of the Brussels butter mountain. Nothing could have been more demoralizing for a university science department and nothing worse for the reputation of science as a course of study. Science education achieved a status within government akin to famine relief and animal welfare. Its value was put beyond question and beyond price. In the 1987 Tory campaign guide, the assertion was axiomatic: 'The country needs more scientists', it said. It arose from 'a clear practical and intellectual recognition in our universities'. What was this recognition? Who says the universities were right? This 'clear practical and intellectual recognition' was not tested in any way.

I would be laughed to scorn if I said that Britain urgently 'needed' more merchant bankers, more lawyers, more dress designers or more journalists and that the government should distort educational priorities to deliver them. Yet courses relevant to each of these subjects are booming at university level in comparison with mathematics and science. Nobody has defined the externalities that make science a uniquely desirable intellectual pursuit in need of government support.

If the economy is crying out for more scientists, market forces dictate that it should pay them higher salaries. It does not. High salaries go to those skilled in finance, law and account-ancy, subjects long neglected by universities. They are derided as 'vocational', yet microbiology or soil chemistry are not so derided. They are lauded as pure science.

British scientists are not, as the lobby claims, 'undervalued' by British industry and commerce. That is to misunderstand the nature of value (and suggests that scientists would be well-advised to study economics). They are valued at their worth. The trouble is that too many of them are being turned out by universities, the market is saturated and thousands each year leave to find employment abroad. Scientists are a great British export, notably to North America. We educate scientists for the rest of the world – much as India educates our doctors – but there is no evidence that we need more of these skills at home. The pressure group Save British Science complains that scientists are shockingly underpaid, which is why they go abroad. That is a value judgement, not a man-power forecast, nor should it become a bureaucratic edict. At the height of the boom in the mid-1980s, the jobs market sought economists, administrators, linguists, lawyers and rewarded them well. Even science-based companies found that they needed fewer scientists – the ones they needed had to be extremely specialized. They most desired graduates who could manage, design, sell, programme computers and account. That message soon passed down the education lad-der. Young people can read the market better than Whitehall or a university science department.

None of this had the slightest impact on policy-making. Ministers redoubled their efforts to make the failed policy work. The frequent revisions to the school curriculum were in the direction of devoting more rather than less time to science and maths. As subjects were dropped from the com-pulsory list after 14 – including history and geography – maths and science retained their priority. The government's School Curriculum and Assessment Authority disregarded the lack of market demand for these subjects as it disregarded the resistance of pupils. The science lobby merely shifted its argument in a different direction. Maths and science were to be valued in themselves as 'alternative cultures', as a training for the mind. The same argument was once used to justify the core status of Latin in the grammar curriculum, centuries after the language had ceased to carry any vocational value.

I regard maths as in much the same category as the classics. It is a mental tool useful for the study of other advanced subjects, albeit a narrow group of them. Certain aspects of science require advanced maths skills. But science is wide ranging and time consuming on the curriculum. Those who want to study it must clearly know maths as a technique, as they need to know other techniques. Likewise economists need to know history. Lawyers need to know political science. The curriculum can be crammed with 'need to know' vocational preliminaries. Maths (other than elementary maths with which I have no quarrel) is difficult, and not needed by anybody who does not intend to pursue the subject as a specialist. Calculating machines can now do most advanced mathematical problems with ease. Teachers seem ashamed at this. It is as if instructors in ploughing or blacksmithing wanted young people to go on learning the traditional skills just in case technology goes backwards rather than forwards. As for training the mind, the arts and the social sciences (Oh for a different name for them!) can be no less taxing and rigorous if well taught.

Nothing was more inadequate than the efforts, long supported by the British Association for the Advancement of Science, to present the science syllabus as a liberal education in itself. This had been resurrected from the 1960s campaign to 'bridge the two cultures', as C. P. Snow called it. The argument for parallelism was not won by Snow then and it was not to be won today. The second law of thermodynamics may have about it an intellectual symmetry, but it is not Jane Austen's *Emma*. It is one thing for talented commentators such as Bronowski, Medawar and more recently Stephen Hawking and Jared Diamond to bring alive the great adventure of scientific history – an adventure in which every child

75

should be initiated. It is quite another to dress mutton up as lamb and hope young people will not notice.

I am suspicious of any academic specialism which demands government protection against market forces. I hear an axe grinding and a closed shop at work. It is ludicrous that science should stand in the education pantheon alongside English and to the exclusion of linguistic skill or a knowledge of the world about us. Geography and history are far more important to a liberal education than maths and science, the way in which people use the earth's resources and organize its communities, the way individuals handle money, citizenship and personal relations. These are true 'core' subjects. I believe the reluctance of educationists to embrace them is not that they are easy or hard but that they are riddled with subjectivity. Science and maths are received wisdom. They are, at least at the school level, about absolutes. The teacher must be right. Parents approve of these subjects for the same reason. There is no danger of them being polluted by repartee, let alone by politics. They can be easily tested. There is virtue in their obscurantism. There is nothing so conservative as a parent's view of the curriculum. 'What was good enough for me is good enough for him.'

The fascination of the modern student with the realm of the imagination, with creativity, art and design, the study of human behaviour and social relationships is not just the hope of finding an easy university option. It is not even that these subjects seem to yield better jobs. I believe it is that they offer the student the chance to test what he or she is being taught in everyday life, the chance to answer back. Students sense these subjects will enrich their lives irrespective of where those lives may lead. Literature and art, politics and economics, psychology and anthropology should not be easy options. They should be as hard as they are in life. They are relevant.

The trouble with science is not in its teaching, nowadays incomparably more effective and enjoyable than it used to be. The trouble is that students do not see the point of it. The subject has been over-sold. Students are voting against

76

it with a myriad ticks on the GCSE and university entrance forms. The consumers of education have defied authority. They have stated what they want and refused to make do with something else. They have taught a Tory cabinet a lesson in free market economics. There is hope for the country yet.

10

CRIME WAVING, OR DROWNING?

THERE IS no human belief as strong as that our parents' youth was a Golden Age. They were optimists and hope sprang eternal. Rules were rules and were disobeyed only from high spirits. Everyman knew his place and every other man respected it. The young dressed to their age and station. Sex was a friendly demon. If there were revolutions they were just ones and meant to hurt nobody. Utopia was just over the horizon. The gods of cynicism had yet to arrive.

Above all, the bonds of community held. People knew and trusted each other. Old Mrs Jones would leave her back door open and the rent was on the table. Mrs Smith would let her daughter walk home across the common. The bicycle was never locked. Crime was always petty and met with a cuff on the ear from the local bobby. 'Thank you, sir,' said the young victim. 'I know I deserved that. I will not steal apples again.' There were no muggers or drug pushers or carjackers or child abusers. A home was a castle that needed no rampart or drawbridge. Those, in a nutshell, were the days.

Such was the Golden Age. During the year of 1993, the British police received visits from no fewer than 150 foreign forces. They came, in ever rising numbers, to see how the world's most famous law enforcers coped with crime. They mentioned in particular Britain's reputation for community policing and crowd control, and the absence of body weapons or armour. The visitors were right to be impressed. That year was marred by two tragic cases of officers killed on duty, one shot the other knifed. But the number of officers assaulted by the public had fallen steadily over the years, despite a rise in the number of 'armed incidents'. The majority of these in Britain do not involve actual weapons but either replicas or a threat to use a non-existent weapon. These are no less a menace, but do not lead to injury.

Six years earlier, in 1987, London had seen almost 5,000 assaults on police men and women. In 1991 the total was down to 3,960 and in 1992 fell further to 1,140, though the 1993 figure was slightly up. Serious assaults leading to injury formed a small percentage of this total, and they also fell, as did the nationwide figures. The number attacked with knives had also fallen over the years, from 63 to 46. As for gun incidents, these were negligible. Most police forces had to search their records to find a case. In London guns were used, and used slightly more often, in the committing of a crime, though rarely against the police, and most were replicas. In 1987 guns were brandished at police on just 20 occasions, in five of which they had actually been fired. In 1992 the figures were 12, with one firing. In 1993 there was a fatal shooting when a constable disturbed a drug ring. An average of 10 police officers are killed in the course of duty in Britain each year, a figure that has been constant for the past 30 years. In 1991 the total was five and in 1992 zero.

The two deaths in 1993 led the Metropolitan Police Commissioner, Sir Paul Condon, to respond by showing his concern for his officers' security. He was aware that policemen did not want to carry guns, nor did the public want them to. Police officers have been shot at, and killed, ever since guns were invented. Brave constables confronted armed robbers and asked them to 'hand over that gun, sonny'. The Craig-Bentley murder was of a policeman. Policemen know that guns cause accidents. An armed and undertrained policeman is a dangerous person. Innocent members of the public have

79

been shot and killed in accidents. As a result, the Metropolitan police reduced the numbers of policemen allowed to use guns, from more than 5,000 in 1980 to just 1,888 in 1993. Whenever police or public are polled, they return majorities of 70 to 80 per cent against routine arming. Criminals feel the same: a poll of unarmed robbers showed 50 per cent saying they would carry guns if they knew the police were armed too. This ratchet effect is known to weigh heavily with police leaders.

Sir Paul made the mildest change available to him. He announced an increase from five to twelve in the number of patrol cars on call in central London with hand guns available in locked boxes. Greater discretion would be given to trained officers in the cars to open the boxes if summoned to an emergency. When asked if this was a step towards the arming of policemen on the beat he unwisely said that it might indeed be a step in that direction. Other chief constables, not wanting to appear soft in the eyes of their staff, said much the same.

The media fell on the story and broadcast it round the world. Without exception they printed a complete falsity, that ordinary policemen on the beat were to carry arms, like foreign forces, in response to rising assaults from the public. The truth was the opposite. Not only were fewer policemen being subjected to assault, armed or otherwise, each year but fewer policemen were being allowed to carry arms in response. All that was really happening was a slight change in the 'rules of engagement'. The reality was good news. Fewer assaults, fewer shootings, fewer armed police, more efficient armed response units. The normal reaction from a police, press and public obsessed with news about crime might have been to cheer. At the very least the politicians might have cheered.

They all did the opposite. Why? The reason, I believe, is that a public subjected to a daily barrage of publicity about the 'crime wave' has lost its ability to absorb and judge statistics. It thus cannot form a balanced view of law and order in the community as a whole. This is dangerous. A crime statistic ceases to be a fact. It defines itself as an upward trend, whose only variant is the rate of its rise. A fall, such as in the total of assaults on policemen, must be some statistical quirk. There cannot be good news about crime. Anecdote, experience, recollection, the syndrome of the Golden Age all conspire in one direction. The world is a worse place than it was before. The young, who commit most recorded crime, are gripped by a novel hostility to society. The body corporate is addicted to bad news and rejects good as alien tissue. John of Gaunt had the best tune. 'This scepter'd isle, dear for her reputation through the world . . . hath made a shameful conquest of itself.'

Let us take a deep breath and look not at the facts – they are mostly unknowable – but at the facts as they are presented to us and as we believe them. The realm of crime in Britain is blessed with not one set of statistics but two. One is published by the Home Office from returns from police forces up and down the country. The other is commissioned by the Home Office itself as a survey of public experience of crime. This is called the British Crime Survey (BCS). One is thus a record of what crimes are reported to the nation's police stations, and how they are entered in crime books. The other is a record of what individuals claim to have experienced over a particular period. Not surprisingly, there is no record of actual crime. Criminals do not check in with the Home Office at the end of each night's shift.

The first thing to say is that the police statistics are almost wholly useless, either as a true record of crime or as a measure of its movement over time. They are simply a record of police station activity. The Home Office's own BCS is scathing about this. 'Police statistics', it states baldly, 'are an unreliable guide to the extent of crime.' They are unreliable both as a snapshot of crime at one moment and as an indication of a trend over time.

We can take two apparently simple examples of this, the figures for manslaughter and rape. Manslaughter has a 99 per cent clear-up rate; bodies are notoriously hard to remove. Homicide has risen steadily but not dramatically over the past four decades but does not appear in the BCS, since the numbers are too small to register on a public opinion poll. The only figures available are thus police figures. Yet police figures are not what they seem. I once asked a chief constable to explain the rise in homicide in his area. Easy, he said, I have more officers and therefore can give more attention to missing persons, of whom there are twice as many as there are homicides. Each year I have fewer missing persons and more homicides: it is really a matter of how many times I want to drag the canal or the dock for a missing prostitute or tramp. Britain's so-called 'murder rate' means nothing.

Rape was recorded nationwide as extremely low after the war. The police tended to record only aggravated, non-domestic cases. Today publicity encourages far more women to report rape. That does not mean the experience of rape is increasing. Rape is too rare to feature in the British Crime Survey and we must depend on police figures. Yet some police stations are known to be sympathetic and have rape counselling units. Others are notoriously unsympathetic. Researchers have shown that more rapes are reported in the former than in the latter – often by a factor as high as ten times. A 'good' police station thus has a high rape figure, a 'bad' one a low figure. We have absolutely no way of knowing if rape is increasing or diminishing in Britain, but the average member of the public believes it to be soaring because of the publicity given to particular cases and to police station statistics. The BCS suggests that assaults on women other than by spouses, friends or neighbours are rare and have remained relatively constant over time.

Other factors can also have an impact on police recorded crime. The closure of a police station cuts reporting: there is seldom a commensurate rise in crime reported at neighbouring stations. Forty per cent of all crime is car crime. Small shifts in no-claims bonuses or other insurance terms can produce large shifts in the reporting to police stations. After a large assembly, such as a carnival or football match, the inclination of police to record lost handbags, pickpocketing or petty theft from shops also varies widely. New products cause surges in crime. Car radios and telephones, like video recorders, are much stolen at present since they are easy to resell. When every car and every home has such equipment, it is likely that the market will fall and thefts will diminish. Videos are nowadays stolen more often than televisions.

Such crimes as vandalism have risen in line with changes in the *de minimis* rules. Is vandalism a crime at £5 in value or at £50? Police forces have varying rules on recording possession of glue (for sniffing), cannabis or offensive weapons. Some are aggressive in arresting under-age homosexuals. By staking out public lavatories they can push up their 'clear-up' rate for sex crimes, which embrace both homosexual acts and rape. Finally, as Roger Graef shows in his book, *Talking Blues*, police forces are regularly shifting arrests from category to category depending on the pressures of the moment.

None of this has anything to do with real crime as experienced in the community. Comparisons with the BCS suggest that police recorded crime may be no more than 20 to 25 per cent of actual crime. Equating police recorded crime with real crime is like counting the pebbles on a beach by only counting the ones on top. Worse, the more counts are made, the more pebbles are found. Each year there are more policemen doing the counting, more telephones enabling crimes to be reported, more insurance policies demanding a police notification, more crimes declared by Parliament. Gloucestershire was shocked one year by a sudden 'crime wave' when one villain confessed to the police 3,000 previous offences of theft. Thames Valley was no less shocked by a 'sex crime soars' headline which followed an enthusiastic raid by a local inspector on a Slough public lavatory. Crime had not risen, only police knowledge of it.

Police recorded crime has risen steadily since figures were first collected in the 1830s. They have risen roughly in line with police employment. Today some 60 per cent of recorded crime is by children under 18. The Children Acts of 1907 and 1933 brought thousands of children who previously had been at the mercy of local constables within the reach of the courts. Both acts led to 'crime waves' that shocked the nation, but were wholly definitional. In the 1930s, a youth leader bewailed the 'passing of parental authority, defiance of pre-war conventions, the absence of restraint, the wildness of extremes, the confusion of unrelated liberties, the wholesale drift away from the churches'. As Geoffrey Pearson wrote in his history of hooliganism, we are tempted to ask, of which period is the writer speaking? In the late 1970s, vandalism rose instantly by over 50 per cent when the Home Office ended the lower value limit on minor incidents. Yet that department continued to publish trends in total crimes since the start of the century. Such trends are meaningless.

Every community in Britain, every housing estate, every school, every factory, every office, is awash with dodgy behaviour. There is petty larceny, cheating, fraud, bribery and corruption. Equipment is stolen, supplies 'go walking', the company is cheated, garments are nicked. Large organizations assume they will lose a certain amount of turnover, as the Inland Revenue and Customs and Excise assume they will fail to recover some of their taxes. Most of this is crime, in the same legislative sense that car crime is crime. The inspector, the policeman, the legislator, the statistician may dip into this morass at will. Millions of teenagers now break the criminal law each night by using cannabis, Ecstasy, amphetamines and acid drugs. Recording, let alone prosecuting, such crimes is a matter of will, like prosecuting all drivers exceeding 30 mph in a built-up area. Even changes from one year to the next are subject to so many variables in police practice and definition as to be beyond generalization.

In my view, the Home Office should not collate police recorded crime figures. They are too unreliable. Politicians and newspapers should not quote them. If police forces wish to publish local figures, whether in the cause of enlightenment or to goad their paymasters into increasing their grants, that is their business. But it does them no credit to lump murder in with shoplifting as 'crime', nor to equate consenting acts between homosexuals with violent rape as 'sex crime'. This simply increases unjustified fear and alarm.

Would I extend this embargo to the British Crime Survey? The answer is no. This complicated and thorough survey of the public's experience of disorder suggests that Britain has four to five times more 'crime' than is known by the police. It also shows a total rising far more slowly, and in some categories falling. The BCS shows crime rising between 1987 and 1992 at 14 per cent over five years, against a police rise of 39 per cent. The BCS figure for the rise in violent crime is 9 per cent against the police's 34 per cent. Even assuming the BCS sample survey is constant, the discrepancy between the two ways of collecting figures is glaring.

The BCS rise in British crime is statistically respectable. But what does it really mean? It conforms to the anecdotal impression, especially among the middle classes, that crime is on an upward trend, though it does not suggest that this trend is rising exponentially towards some social collapse. We need to know whether the increase is a function of rising expectations of social order, of rising prosperity, or of some shift in social behaviour especially among the young which might, or might not, be susceptible to corrective action. We must understand what a rise in crime consists of before we can treat it.

I believe that nobody really knows if crime is really rising, in the sense of more people operating outside the norms of decent social behaviour. We are here in the realm not of statistics but of anthropology. We are delving into our own feelings about our vulnerability and that of our possessions. We are examining the public and private spaces around us. We are reacting differently to those who frighten or upset us, including those we know and love.

Whenever we scratch the surface of collective behaviour, we unearth a new level of misdemeanour which the community once took in its stride but which it now files away as crime. Two thirds of all crime is stealing. Half of this involves cars and the rest mostly videos, televisions, cameras and money. These goods are more widespread than ever before. It would be odd if more of them did not get stolen. It would be odd if opportunist thieves who once confined their attention to the family silver of the rich did not now regard every house as having pickings worth the effort.

Most Britons leave their most valuable possession, their car, unguarded in a public street. In working class England between the wars, such carelessness with valuable property would have been considered lunatic. (Americans keep their cars in garages and experience less auto-crime as a result.) Inside these cars are left highly marketable radios and telephones. Thefts of cars and from cars rose by a half over the 1980s: so did the ownership of cars. In Britain such crime embraces 40 per cent of reported offences.

Many wealthy and even not so wealthy people go further. They buy second homes, often in isolated places in the country, fill them with consumer durables and broadcast to the local community that they will be left unattended for five days a week. In the old days, a police station regarded a house unattended for a week as so at risk of burglary that it would be entered on a list at the police station. None of this excuses the undoubted rise in rural burglary. It does help explain why it has become so widespread in the south-east of England over the past decade.

I believe most property crime is not a function of some new evil among Britain's young people. It is a function of boredom, unemployment and ease of opportunity. A youth with nothing else to do and no easy way of making money is more likely to steal than one with a job. This stands to reason. In the 1980s, circumstances were conducive to a rise in such crime: a widening gulf between those in and out of work and rising ownership of tradable consumer goods. Those with property valued it more highly. They insured it, reported it when stolen and remembered its loss when asked by a BCS surveyor. They also noted, and talked about, rises in property crime in one area but did not notice its decline in another (such as central London). It is not surprising that acquisitive crime, as the BCS terms it, rose 85 per cent over the decade of the 1980s – sad but not surprising.

Now violence. The British Crime Survey shows this category rising by much less than property crime, by 15 per cent over the decade. It is almost impossible to 'fix' this statistic. A sociologist will assert that our tolerance of violence is falling and that this is a good thing. Marginal incidents – a brawl outside a pub, a domestic beating, an outbreak of football hooliganism – that would once have been deplored as high spirits are now recalled as crimes. Publicans in working class areas of the north used at the turn of the century to have a club or shotgun behind the bar to drive out rowdy drunks on a Saturday night. Today they will simply call the police and a crime is registered. As Geoffrey Pearson records, crowd and pitch violence were frequent features of early football matches. In the 1920s, knives and clubs were used in fights between Arsenal and Spurs supporters. *The Times* in the early 1930s reported that 'terror gangs of bag snatchers' were leaving elderly ladies wounded in the gutter. It reported a 90 per cent rise in muggings of women between 1925 and 1929. Returning soldiers and the 'lawless young' were blamed, as they were in similar 'crime waves' reported after the Second World War.

It is hardly possible to disentangle an actual rise in violence in Britain from a declining tolerance towards it. Violence between individuals exists in all societies and has done so for all time. Most violence is between individuals who know one another. The two principal venues for violence are the home and the street (with roughly 500,000 BCS incidents in each). Another 400,000 incidents are in a pub or club. In the home almost all victims are women, in the street or pub almost all are men. Women almost invariably know their assailant, men claim in 70 per cent of cases not to know him. Drink is a factor in over half the home, street and pub violence. The extraordinary thing about these totals is how little they have changed over the years. The latest survey shows a slight fall in violence between strangers and the rise concentrated chiefly on domestic violence. Yet this rise could itself be the result of our treating domestic violence as less normal, more criminal, these days. As with property crime, changing attitudes to personal violence appear to go some way to explaining the rise in the BCS figures.

A sceptic might propose an obvious remedy for the 'crime wave'. First he would cut reported crime at a stroke by

87

reversing the definitional drift of the past quarter century. He would reintroduce a *de minimis* level for vandalism, say at damage costing £100 to repair. The sceptic might end the insuring of unlocked cars, make an excess payment compulsory and even end the practice of using the police to give insurance companies a free claim-monitoring service. This would make owners more careful of their cars and eliminate the bulk of reported thefts from static motor vehicles. Assaults by drunks on drunks in licensed premises could be 'decriminalized'. The decriminalization of homosexual acts by 16 to 18 year olds and of soft drug possession would also reduce the figures. None of this would affect wrong-doing as such. But the reported crime figures would plummet and, such is public psychology, the public would feel safer, use the streets more and probably *be* safer as a result.

As far as the BCS figures are concerned, public education should warn young men – the group most at risk of violence – about the real danger of pubs and clubs at night. Women should have more ready counselling on domestic violence, and more plentiful refuges. Second homes should be made more secure. Alcohol is a devastating public menace, and appears to be as much a contributory cause of violent crime as unlocked cars and unattended houses are of property crime. It should be far more highly taxed and its consumption in public places restricted.

Nothing would be more helpful than for the press not to disseminate straightforward untruths about crime. It was widely asserted during the coverage of the Bulger murder in 1993 that young people in Britain were increasingly turning to violent crime. Certainly there are gangs of youngsters in the tougher inner city areas, involved in thieving and drug-running. There always have been. They often plea-bargain when caught by admitting hundreds of previous offences, thus wildly distorting property figures for the locality.

The Home Office figures are clear in this matter: the number of males under 18 arrested, cautioned or convicted fell over the six-year period from 1985 to 1991 from 219,000 to 149,000, only half the fall being attributable to the decline in the size of the relevant age group. 'Known offenders' under the age of 14 fell by 43 per cent. These figures appeared nowhere in the coverage of the Bulger case that I could find. The reason, I have no doubt, is that most journalists and most readers simply could not bring themselves to believe them. The statistics must be lying. Yet why then do these same people implicitly believe police reported crime figures – that really are lying? The only answer, I repeat, is that crime is a subject on which the public yearns to believe the worst. The Golden Age syndrome must hold good.

The media say that highlighting bad news about crime and other social evils helps cure them. This is rubbish. In the first place, crime is highlighted by the media not as any public service but because 'crime-scare' stories have a quasi-pornographic appeal to readers. Television companies know this only too well. Hence the rash of programmes purporting to reconstruct real crimes and even rerun videos of them in progress. What is dangerous and socially demoralizing is that the emphasis on crime in the media, on violent crime and on violence against women in particular, increases fear. Since fear is felt by far more people than experience actual crime, indeed by almost everybody, fuelling fear beyond what is justified by risk is inexcusable. And whatever is happening to crime in Britain, there is no doubt from survey material that fear of crime is rising rapidly.

Women are the chief victims of this. A 1994 MORI poll showed that 80 per cent of women under the age of 25 'feared being raped'. Forty per cent feared to go out at night. This is despite the extremely small chance of their being attacked in a public place ever in their lives, as compared for instance to their being injured in their car or wounded by someone they know at home. A recent report in Leicester found that 30 per cent of women not only feared rape but expected a sexual attack in the coming year, an expectation with no basis in reality. The most uncommon attack is a physical assault on an old lady in her own home. The risk is statistically insignificant. Yet such is the coverage given to each case that old women are said to 'live in fear of their lives' on housing estates the length of the land. The community feels a natural horror at attacks on frail elderly people. The elderly themselves feel vulnerable because of their frailty. But what purpose is served by never mentioning the low risk of attack while sensationalizing each case? We merely imprison old people in an irrational fear. We, not the criminals, are the ones blighting their lives.

Such is the publicity given to attacks on women that most consciously allow it to influence their daily behaviour. Being attacked by a stranger, being raped by an unknown person or assaulted on public transport occurs so rarely as to be unmeasurable in the British Crime Survey. The transport police claim that crime on the London Underground has been falling for seven years consecutively. I doubt if many Londoners either know this or would believe it if told. Yet they would believe such statistics if they showed a steady rise. Fear has become the stereotype. It is used by manufacturers to bombard women in particular with marketing of personal alarms, car phones, video systems, steel grilles and karate lessons. Fear is big money. It depends on publicity being given to the concept of a perpetual crime wave.

An obsession with a 'crime wave' is in part a function of age. Perhaps I suffer from inverted prejudice, but I find the gullibility of age even worse than the bumptious iconoclasm of youth. Each generation seems to excuse its own inadequacy by claiming that the next is less caring, less intelligent, more ugly and certainly more criminal than any that went before. Evidence to the contrary must be faulty. This daftness only becomes dangerous when it leads to bad policy. Every three or four years, weak Home Secretaries come up with a new idea for 'getting tough with the young thugs'. The result is that Britain incarcerates more young people than does any other country in Europe. It has introduced, successively, borstals, approved schools, young offenders' institutions and short sharp shock camps. In 1993, the Home Secretary said he would build a national network of secure units for 400 or so tough cases. The annual cost would be high, about £2,000 per inmate a week. Since the reoffending rate after attendance in prison is double that after non-custodial community orders, the deal must be a bad one for the taxpayer and the public.

Criminality is still uncommon in Britain. Most young men have some brush with the law in their teens and early twenties, usually over car use and what are known as lifestyle offences such as drug possession. As they mature, they turn away from wrongdoing and deplore the behaviour of the next generation. Crime contrives to be abnormal and yet common among young people. Robust, confident communities understand this abnormality, contain it and minimize the damage it may do to their cohesion. The task of politicians and the media is not to exaggerate the abnormality but to keep it in proportion. Crime is fought where it exists. Fear of crime must be fought everywhere. Above all it must be fought when fuelled by partial and misleading statistics. Such statistics are worse than lies. They rot more than the mind. They rot society.

11

THE LAST TALLY-HO?

DICKENS WAS right. There is, he said, 'a passion for hunting deeply implanted in the human breast.' Tolstoy and Trollope both agreed. They sent their farmers and factors, their parsons and politicians galloping through the autumn mist. All were bearing witness to something in the countryman's breast that the townsman cannot fully comprehend: the heat of the chase, the thrill of speed, the risk of injury, the turmoil of the kill, in which class distinction vanishes. It is man against beast, the survival of the fittest down the ages.

I do not hunt. I do not like hunting. I derive no pleasure from the killing of living things and am suspicious of the mental state of those who do. But I acknowledge that nothing so furiously divides left and right, macho and wimp, above all town and country. Nor is dislike the same as disallow. My feelings are not the feelings of Everyman. The basis on which I translate my disagreement into legal compulsion must extend beyond personal aversion. Hunting is a sport practised since time began and in every corner of the world. Its controversies are global, from stag and foxhunting in Britain to the pursuit of elephant and rhinoceros in Africa. They are also interwoven with the politics of wildlife conservation.

A favourite question asked of philosophy students is, 'Do

animals have rights?' The correct answer is no: rights are what humans have evolved, or invented, to order their supremacy on earth after conquering other forms of life. A more correct answer is, no but . . . We do accord animals some rights, indeed we protect many by means of the law. We do so on a vague hierarchy of anthropomorphic qualities. I can kill a cat without reporting it to the police, but not a dog. Our love of dogs and horses makes the killing of either species abhorrent, even to those who take pleasure in killing animals such as foxes and stags. If the Master of the Quorn were told that a spaniel hunt or a Shetland pony kill was taking place on his land, he would doubtless don his anorak, collect his aniseed and turn hunt saboteur.

Many people draw a distinction between killing to eat, killing to conserve nature, and killing for pleasure. Hunters draw no such distinction. They point out that all three have been present in the countryside since time began. None the less the breeding of pheasants so that wealthy town-dwellers can down them with shot is to many countrymen obscene. It has nothing to do with culling or pest control. The bursting of a deer's lungs in the course of a chase by hounds can be equally offensive. Yet there is no more than a fine philosophical distinction between such killing and the methodical slaughter of cows, sheep and pigs for food, sometimes unwanted food that is stored and burnt.

Albert Schweitzer said, in reference to all the living things of Africa, that a 'compassion for all that is called life is the beginning and foundation of morality'. But like many moralists, Schweitzer tackled the easy questions but not the hard ones. Would he have come to the same conclusion about capital punishment, about abortion, about the eating of meat? Defining the boundaries of life challenges our reason. It taxes our concept of ourself and our relationship to the organic world. The moral philosopher, Jonathan Glover, points out in his book *Causing Death and Taking Lives* that it is absurd to treat the killing of any living thing as 'intrinsically wrong', if for no other reason than that most of us do it all the time.

Religious sects, such as the Indian followers of Jainism,

maintain that it is evil to kill even a fly or an ant. Who knows what – or who – it might have been in a former incarnation? This leads to a limited lifestyle. Even the act of walking along a country path can involve an ethical torment. Killing some living things is for most of us what philosophers call a situational ethic. We justify it morally because the alternative is inconvenient. None the less, says Glover, we continue to regard killing as wrong in the absence of some good reason for doing it, such as to keep our bodies functioning or to resist aggression in war. A sadist may delight in maiming and slaughtering, and a film producer may find profit in glorifying such people, but we do not accept that as justification. Where a killer is pulling wings off butterflies, we shudder. Where his victim is a protected animal we invoke the law to stop him.

In extremis I would kill for my country. I would be irrationally violent if anybody harmed someone I loved. If some pest must be eliminated or some creature killed for the table, I want the deed done swiftly and with a minimum of pain. We may not know how animals feel or think. But I sense some shared consciousness with other mammals, including fear and pain. Nor, surely, is hunting a plausible prophylactic against worse violence by those practising it. A member of the Beaufort Hunt is not staving off a repressed vocation as a serial killer.

I thus may kill to eat but not derive pleasure from the act. But what of the third leg of the argument, killing to conserve both animals and their habitats? In Britain, hunting and shooting are not just part of the past of the countryside. They are claimed as its future. The British countryside is now threatened by forces more devastating than any since industrialization. The collapse of farm price support must eventually undermine the use of the countryside as a food factory. Other parts of the world will undercut less efficient British farms. The days of the arable agribusiness, the sheep run and the cow pasture are numbered. Hence the trend to leisure farming and the new threat to the fields and hedgerows of Britain from suburbanization, from golf courses, caravan sites, theme parks and chalet camps. For any lover of the landscape, a traditional use that keeps it as it is must be better than these.

Hunting is money. Grouse moors, pheasant covets, fields and hedges tended for the passage of horses mean landscape conserved. There may be more humane methods of culling Britain's booming fox and deer populations, which thrive on proximity to human habitation. But there are few more profitable ones. Up goes £100, bang goes 50p, down comes £5 may seem strange economics but it is true, and it keeps thousands of acres of wood and field in being. If the cry of the hunt and crackle of the shoot can stave off the ruin of the British landscape until some new salvation is devised, my ethics become situational. I might prefer it otherwise, but beggars cannot be moral chosers.

The identical dilemma can be seen in Africa, over the hunting of the elephant. This magnificent animal ranks with the blue whale, the panda and the gorilla as what conservationist jargon calls a charismatic megaspecies. It attracts heated argument. That heat is reported in *At the Hand of Man* by the American journalist Raymond Bonner. Clearly a lover of elephants, Bonner argues for the encouragement of big game hunting. He is for selling ivory. He is content to see the residences of American tycoons adorned with elephant heads, tiger rugs and rhinoceros horns. His reason is straightforward. The promotion of big game hunting in Africa is, for the time being, the only way of preserving these species. Politics will never do it. Without commercial hunting, the animals will become extinct or be confined to breeding zoos. They will go the way of the mammoth and the sabre-tooth tiger.

Bonner's enemy is unreason. He is an elephant enthusiast and watches these beasts wandering the bush, in Karen Blixen's words, 'as if they had an appointment at the end of the world'. But he has also experienced the cesspit of elephant politics and come out spitting with anger. He seems convinced that the arrogance of his countrymen towards African attitudes to conservation is a threat to the elephant's future on that continent. In recent years it has been rare to open a children's magazine or wildlife brochure without seeing heart-rending photographs of mutilated elephants, villainous poachers and bloodstained ivory. The pictures are always accompanied by appeals for money – money that is never to be sent to an address in Africa.

I once visited a game reserve in Botswana and encountered nothing but fury at this campaign. Elephants in Africa are not dying out nor ever have been. They are not endangered. In some countries their numbers are dwindling, but overall elephant numbers are increasing. Since they are a menace to farm crops, farmers are naturally happy to see them killed and turn a blind eye to poachers who wish to profit from illicit ivory. As a result, elephant numbers have recently been falling in East Africa, where the most intense preservation lobbying is concentrated. They have been increasing in southern Africa where shooting and (covertly) the amassing of ivory stocks has been taking place. Botswana's elephant numbers doubled in the 1980s.

Bonner's case is that Africans must be able to make money out of elephants and other big game, or they will sooner or later wipe them out. Poor people who live side by side with wild animals must have a financial interest in their survival. Tourism is not a sufficient interest. A game park may protect a few herds for visitors, as does Woburn in Britain. But the twenty Land Rovers that now encircle every lion pride in Kenya destroy the habitat and the food chain and bring little revenue to local farmers. The latter have little incentive to help conserve the beasts. Soon the reserves become no more than guarded safari parks. If elephants are to survive in anything like a natural state, Africans must want to protect them and the ecological diversity that supports them.

The elephant must be exploited as a crop. If the owner of land inhabited by elephants has too many elephants for it to support, he must cull them. They are pests to his crops and his trees. Since the elephant must be culled it makes no sense to deny the farmer the money from the cull, in hunting fees and in ivory. The higher this income, the more the farmer will accept the elephant as a source of livelihood.

Bonner maintains that the biggest enemy of the elephant is the elephant lobby. Until 1988, every leading conservationist backed what is termed the sustainable utilization of African wildlife. Wild animals were to be treated as part of the local ecology, which meant treating them as part of the local economy. One painful example of what this meant was the shooting of the last herd of 100 elephants in Rwanda in the late 1970s. The African Wildlife Foundation (AWF), among others, concluded that the elephants, confined into an ever smaller area, were rapidly destroying the Rwandan forest. In doing so, they were destroying the habitat of Africa's last colony of wild gorillas. It was elephants or gorillas. The gorillas took 'species precedence'.

In 1989 the tide turned. Responsible wildlife organizations were under attack from militant animal rights groups emanating mostly from America. International conferences saw white militants pitted against white zoologists. Africans were little more than bystanders. At the 1989 Lausanne conference – these arguments are conducted in the most comfortable locations – East African delegates eager for aid were browbeaten by American lobbyists. They deserted the cause of sustainable utilization and turned militant. The elephant was declared endangered, though it was not, and the trade in ivory was banned. Southern African states opposed the ban but were forced into line. Zimbabwe, with a creditable elephant conservation record, was allegedly threatened with the loss of American aid.

Bonner charts the evolution of the ban. It had little to do with elephant conservation and everything to do with the mechanics of fund-raising. He reports an AWF fund-raising consultant 'screaming' for endangered status because of the publicity value. There was no money in America in strategic culling. There was certainly no money in arguing for cross-subsidy from ivory taxes into elephant conservation. Mangled corpses, cries of animal holocaust and genocide, phoney statistics of 'extinction in ten years' had by the end of the 1980s become the most successful fund-raising campaign in conservation history. The elephant ousted even the panda in the

97

affections of children. The World Wildlife Fund was blud-geoned into joining the campaign. The 1989 ivory ban had an immediate short term impact. The world price of ivory fell and African countries lost some $50m in foreign currency. In Nairobi, $3m-worth of ivory which might have financed Kenya's impoverished elephant conservation programme, was burnt as a publicity stunt by Richard Leakey.

Were there a world market for ivory, Africans would breed elephant and rhinoceros for profit, as Americans breed alli-gators and Britons breed grouse. Both alligators and grouse have, in the past, been threatened with extinction. Hunting elephant is still permitted in some countries as a form of culling. This has not only brought revenue into local conser-vation, it brings far more and at less cost to the habitat than a hundred camera safari tourists. To ban the ivory trade and oppose the hunter is thus to deliver a double blow to the conservation of the African bush. It threatens it with financial starvation.

For the West to impose on Africans a moral code that impoverishes them and endangers their wildlife is hypocriti-cal. I wonder how Britons would react to an African demand that grouse and venison be banned from London's restaurant menus. The argument for permitting the hunting of the elephant is, like that for hunting grouse and stags, to protect these animals and their surroundings from destruction. Per-haps one day every African elephant and every British stag will be tagged and corralled and forced into a zoo shed at night, where breeding and numbers will be controlled. Per-haps that will obviate the need to cull. I suppose some philos-opher will then tell me that zoos are immoral and unnatural places in which to incarcerate these animals for their survival. For the time being, I am persuaded that the hunter has his rightful place in the conservationist crusade.

12

GRANDMOTHER MUMS

OF ALL the stories that have warmed my heart in recent years none was warmer than that of the Christmas Day present from modern medicine to a unnamed 59-year-old British woman. The present was twins. By giving birth on a day without much news, the mother was assured a lively press. She had her press, but not the sort for which she might have hoped.

What to a mother was a moment of joy, to assorted pundits and publicity-seekers was a moment of outrage. The woman had 'defied nature'. She had been helped to her pregnancy by hormone treatment and *in vitro* fertilization (IVF) from a doctor in a Rome clinic. He had helped some 45 women over the age of 50 to have pregnancies with eggs donated by younger women. Her action qualified for the word controversial, and wherever the media declare a controversy, politicians and others must be found to declare an outrage. There is no shortage of such people over the Christmas break.

They were swift in coming forward. Dr John Marks, formerly chief of the British Medical Association, spoke of his 'horror' at the case. He suggested that it 'bordered on the Frankenstein syndrome'. The word sent shivers of joy through Fleet Street sub-editors. The boundary that divides a good news from a bad news story may be a narrow one.

But once drawn, there is no holding back. The woman was branded a modern witch, to be set in a ducking stool and subjected to torture by soundbite. Dr Stuart Horner of the BMA's ethics committee came out against her on the grounds that such children would have to experience parents 'of a wholly foreign generation'. A BBC newscast bewailed the fact that the British government was 'powerless to stop a woman deciding to have a child'. Phone-in programmes were jammed with comment, letters columns likewise. Most of it was critical, though I caught one middle-aged woman on the radio calling in and just shouting 'Hurrah!'

Well ahead of the pack was the Health Secretary, Virginia Bottomley, popping up on the Christmas television screen time and again to voice not her congratulations to the lucky mother but her unspecified 'grave reservations'. She would get her European health minister colleagues to act on the matter in the New Year. Those whom newspapers were able to reach over the holiday gave Mrs Bottomley a lesson in political dignity. The Italian, Dutch and Spanish ministers all suggested that this was a purely personal matter and they had not the slightest intention of commenting. However, a Vatican expert in Rome was more forthright. 'The psychological phases of maternity coincide naturally with the physiological phases,' said Father Gonzalo Miranda of the Catholic University. He opposed the work of fertility clinics as part of the search for the 'complete good of every human being, which includes the need to avoid forced situations and unpredictable outcomes.'

A hundred clinics in Italy were believed to be offering fertility treatment to older women. The country is one of the few in Europe that does not have formal controls on clinics and has therefore become a haven for women desperate for unorthodox treatment. An Italian woman of 62, also a patient of the same Rome doctor, had already attracted publicity for becoming pregnant (and later giving birth) after a son had been killed in a car crash. 'If only you knew what darkness there is in this house,' she was reported as saying. 'The love I will give this baby could not be given by a 20-year-old mother. If I died the child would be loved by my cousins and nephews as much as I would love him. The whole village of Casino already loves this baby.' She appears not to have considered the possibility of it being a girl.

There is no medical reason why the sperm of a 45-year-old man and the egg of a 25-year-old woman, implanted into a healthy 59-year-old woman, should not produce normal twins. Certainly it is unusual. Of course the children of such parents will have a different upbringing from the children of 19-year-olds, 29-year-olds or 39-year-olds. Their parents are older. But all parents are older than their children. They are all of a different generation. This mother would not have required an electronic calculator to work out how old she would be as her children grew up. She certainly did not need the BMA or the Health Secretary to go on television to do the sums for her. Nor did she need a squawk of agony aunts to tell her that twins at any age are tiring.

A respected French professor none the less dismissed her pregnancy with horror. Professor Jean-François Mattei said that 'the woman has been reduced to an incubator and the child to an object. Pregnancy is a physical and psychological trial for a woman, and nature considers that once a woman reaches menopause her body is no longer able to assure pregnancy without unforeseeable risks.' I wonder if the learned professor would take the same view of operations to unblock fallopian tubes or replace worn-out hip joints? A doctor pleading for nature to be allowed to take its course is a bizarre thing indeed. All pregnancy has 'unforeseeable risks', including that of deformed children in mature mothers. Doctors do not ban such pregnancies. They regard their Hippocratic Oath as requiring them to assist rather than obstruct the treatment of a mother. The appeal to psychology looks even more ominous, as if the increasing physical fitness of older women cannot be permitted to get in the way of a prejudice against mature pregnancy. The concept of mental unfitness for motherhood opens a new realm of disapproval and regulation. Presumably mothers of any age can be deemed psychologically unfit to have children, even by their partners.

Perhaps the most sensible response to the Christmas twins came from the gynaecologist, Ian Croft. He pointed out that conception does occasionally occur after 50. If it occurs naturally in some women, why should it not be assisted in others? We already assist conception in young infertile mothers. He pleaded in a letter to *The Times*, 'Let us not have an overreaction to a rare event by imposing an upper age limit.' Why should it be seen as a 'natural disaster' for any couple to have a desired child when science could enable them to do so?

The reaction to the Christmas births was riddled with confusion. Most glaring was the hypocrisy of assuming that a mature man is perfectly capable of responsible fatherhood – indeed is often congratulated on it – while a mature woman is incapable of motherhood. As if to justify this prejudice, distinctions were drawn between the mother's role and the father's, the latter's being regarded as progressively superfluous as a child grows up but the mother's being crucial. This distinction is specious. It is also denied by the nuclear family lobby which claims 'families without fathers' are morally and socially deficient.

A similar confusion surrounded the status of the egg. *In vitro* fertilization is widely considered acceptable for parents of 'child-bearing age', even where one parent is infertile and a donor egg or sperm is used. More complicated moral issues appear to surround the genetic background of the egg or sperm. For instance a black mother attracted criticism for using a white woman's egg as part of a successful *in vitro* fertility treatment. Yet similar criticism does not attend fostering or adoption of children by genetically unrelated parents. Step parenthood may have its problems, but nobody claims there to be a moral issue of whether or not a step parent can responsibly bring up a child that is not biologically his or her own.

With each pushing out of the boundary of what is considered unnatural, the personal freedom of parents must contend with conventions of taste. Doctors speak of what they call the 'yuk' factor. Ways round the acute shortage of eggs for fertilization have suffered from this, including their transplantation from cadavers after accidents and from aborted foetuses. Both sources are apparently suitable for IVF. The news announced in 1994 that ways have been found to freeze unfertilized eggs – only fertilized ones could at present be frozen – might end this controversy. A woman would be able to freeze her eggs when she is young and, in theory, make use of them at any stage of her life when she chooses to have children. This should obviate the need of mature mothers to use donor eggs. It should also greatly reduce the risk of a deformed foetus developing in mature mothers.

I am on the side of personal freedom. Science has given women the opportunity to exercise far greater control over their lives than used to be the case. Contraception, intra-uterine surgery, fertility drugs, abortion, hormone replacement therapy have all, in various ways, revolutionized sexual practice and family planning. These advances, all made in the past quarter century, are collectively one of the wonders of the modern world. They have liberated women's sexuality from the terror of unwanted pregnancy, and potentially liberated millions of infertile couples from the sadness of impotence. *In vitro* fertilization falls into this category.

Certainly the welfare of the resulting children is a reasonable concern of society, and thus possibly of government. That is well short, however, of a Health Secretary declaring, as did Mrs Bottomley, that a 'British woman has no right to a child' as if this right had been assumed by ministers of the Crown. When *in vitro* fertilization started – its first triumph was the birth of Louise Brown in 1978 – a Human Fertilization and Embryology Authority was set up. The authority went to some lengths not to propose new laws on IVF, despite being constantly invited to do so by ministers. It sought to inspect and licence clinics and stimulate debate on advances in genetic medicine.

A particular taboo seems to afflict the process of childbirth in Britain. It is as if every conception was a social act, requiring the intervention of public policy to regulate any rights or obligations of parents. What was so extraordinary about the Christmas twins was that those who rushed to judgment had not the slightest knowledge of the mother, who wisely took legal steps to protect her privacy. Most did not contest her right to seek help in achieving fertility. Women are allowed to travel and presumably make use of whatever services are legally available in foreign countries. The pontificators judged instead whether she would be a 'good mother' and decided that she would not.

The world is full of children of unconventional parents. It is full of children brought up by grandparents or other relatives as old as the couple in question. In the past, grandparents were often the only active custodians for children whose parents were dead, abroad, separated or working in service. Natural birth does not mean a conventional or necessarily a happy upbringing. Unconventional upbringing is not necessarily unhappy. Children throughout history have defied the nature of their childhood and made their own way in the world, scars and all. Kipling's most heart-rending short story, 'Baa, Baa Black Sheep', drew on his own childhood in England separated from his parents in India. How Kipling might have longed for a mother like the 62-year-old Sicilian whose son would be a 'cherub and a gift of God'. In my experience, older couples tend to make more stable and more loving homes than younger ones. There are fewer divorces among couples in their fifties than among those in their twenties. The pontificators might more usefully have directed their scorn at teenage mothers, whose offspring are statistically far more likely to grow up in an unstable family. Such motherhood is blessed because it is youthful. Like early marriage it is encouraged by the church and lauded by the maternity industry.

I believe much of the criticism was rooted not in any coherent philosophy of parenthood but in envy. Most couples plan their families on the basis that the wife would be past childbearing by her early forties. Here was a woman upsetting the apple-cart. Why should she have this lucky break when others had had to call it a day? The proclaimed concern for the status of children with elderly parents was no more than a cover. The woman was having it both ways, a career and a family. It was unfair. All credit to a lady in her sixties who wrote to me saying that she and her husband had married when she was in her early fifties. They had often talked of how much they would have loved a child if only science had found a way. Had she known what she now knew, she would unquestionably have joined the mother in such an operation. 'I am overjoyed for her,' she added.

If age is to be a criterion by which the state regulates a woman's access to fertility treatment, other criteria might soon creep onto the agenda. Perhaps decisions on whether to continue with the pregnancy of deformed foetuses might be taken out of a mother's hands. Those with inherited genetic irregularities such as haemophilia might, in some way, be discouraged from having natural children. There might be a case for encouraging abortions among teenage mothers, given the evidence that children of such mothers are likely to experience a broken home. To those who gaze on each advance in scientific medicine and say, where will it all end, I reply, where will each advance in meddling interference from government end?

I prefer to put such thoughts out of mind and reflect again on the happiness of that 59-year-old mother. She knew what she wanted. She knew that science could give it to her. No public money was involved. No law was broken. Nobody's rights were infringed. Nobody directly involved was anything but overjoyed. So what business have the rest of us to intrude on her happiness?

13

KISSING AND TELLING

BRITISH PUBLIC life offers much stale bread. It seldom offers circuses. But when it does, the circus comes in style. Round the ring dances a glittering cast of aristocratic spies, neurotic royals and adulterous politicians. They are attended by a pack of salivating reporters all in caps and bells. The show adds greatly to the gaiety of the nation and has become an integral part of Britain's image abroad. It has little to do with justice or good government.

In March 1994 the Chief of the Defence Staff, Sir Peter Harding, was revealed by an *agent provocateur* for a newspaper as having had an affair with the former wife of a Tory MP. The lady had sought to entrap him for money with the aid of a publicity agent. She gave some of his letters to the *News of the World*. Sir Peter was performing the most senior military job in the country. The Defence Secretary affirmed that he had 'total confidence in his (Sir Peter's) professional abilities'. His competence was attested by his military colleagues and by those who knew him in the press. Sir Peter felt obliged to resign. He immediately became a 'warrior felled by the gutter press', a 'soldier of great distinction' and a 'gentleman of the old school'. A soldier had died as if on active service. This was not quite the funeral of Sir John Moore at

Corunna. But drums were heard and funeral notes as his corpse to the rampart they hurried.

Sometime before Sir Peter's accident, the Prime Minister, John Major, had a not dissimilar misfortune. He was described in the *New Statesman* and a fringe periodical as the victim of unsubstantiated rumours concerning a caterer much used for Downing Street parties. In British libel law it is not enough to describe a rumour as unsubstantiated or even untrue, if the purpose of doing so is patently to put the rumour into circulation. This was clearly intended by the publications involved. They then aggravated the sin by refusing to apologize on the grounds that, in saying there was no evidence of truth, they had nothing for which to apologize. Mr Major and his lawyers took a different view and issued writs for libel. As with Sir Peter's resignation, a story that might have remained an item in the more squalid corners of the press, was promptly elevated to national prominence.

Public figures should strive to keep their private lives their own. Often this is not possible. When a private matter has become public, they should struggle at least to disregard the tabloid press and not make mountains out of molehills. A molehill is rightly defined in the dictionary as 'a small mound of dirt thrown up by a burrowing insectivorous mammal'. Such mounds infuriate the owners of suburban lawns, but most experts advise treading them softly back into the ground and waiting for summer. Gassing or the use of explosives seems to encourage them. Injunctions and writs for libel are undignified and usually counterproductive. In the case of a Prime Minister, the authority of his word alone should be enough to end a false rumour. If that is not enough and the law has to be prayed in aid, the Prime Minister's credibility is diminished. When the Prince of Wales's private life was inundated with rumours in 1994, he went on television and calmly stated what was true and what was false. It was a bold coup and it appeared to work. He neither sued nor capitulated to his tormentors. He faced them down.

Gossip is the Puck of politics, that 'merry wanderer of the night', seeking dew drops and hanging pearls in every cowslip's ear. He attends on every person in the public eye and does so for the duration. He sends both thrills and chills down the spine of public and victim alike. 'I am afraid you should probably see this,' says the ministerial aide, holding a newspaper cutting circled in yellow ink like a stinking fish. She struggles to conceal her mirth behind a look of deep concern. The minister feels the panic rising in his gorge. Is it about a colleague, requiring him to shake his head in mock sorrow? Or is he himself the victim? If so he will suffer the sickness in the stomach, the glances of his outer office, the averted eyes of his colleagues and the tear-stained face of his wife.

Unlike Puck, gossip cannot be summoned and dismissed at will. It is the reminder of the glummer side of politics, the eagerness to bring the mighty down, to kick them into the gutter. Hesiod, first pedlar of useful maxims, remarked that 'no gossip ever dies; it has a kind of divinity'. If gossip-mongers wish to enhance their tales with the glamour of publication, then a politician should show amused contempt. He should treat gossip as the pain of a living reputation. Those who seek fame must accept that they will be gossip's object, not its *répétiteur*. They must deny untruths and find ways to live through truths and half-truths. If they are so sensitive as to permit gossip 'to affect the conduct of my work' to use a much-quoted phrase, they are not up to the job.

A prime minister cannot do anything without it becoming generally known – any more than can an American president. A prime minister still under 50 and with a spark of life in him, will find his acquaintances of the opposite sex subject to scrutiny. If his tired visage and hangdog demeanour come strangely alive when he sits next to a pretty woman it will be noted. He cannot sing, dance, collapse, cry, make friends or enemies without the fact entering the discourse of an ever widening circle. If one thing was certain about Mr Major, it was that sooner or later people would gossip about him. The motive force of a rumour has nothing to do with its truth or falsity. It has to do with the importance of the people about whom it is told. Fame diminishes the importance of accuracy.

There is little currency in a salacious story about a vicar or a psychologist if it is not true. Tell it of a film star or a footballer and the fact that somebody might think it true intrigues the listener. Tell it of a prime minister or an heir to the throne and new factors come into play. 'It can't be true!' is overwhelmed by 'Oh let it be true!' Such mooring ropes as 'allegedly', 'it is rumoured', 'I doubt if it is true but . . .' all snap, as gossip's balloon soars upwards.

I believe in libel laws. A person damaged by a published falsehood should have the right to demand that the newspaper prove the truth of its statement. The burden of proof should be on the defendant not on the victim. Nor should it make any difference, as it does in America, if the victim is a public figure. Public office does not strip anyone of their civil rights. It does, however, require that public figures rise above the swamp – otherwise known as acquiring a thick skin. Most politicians develop such a skin as part of the job. They must absorb the banter of the House of Commons and the television studio. Mr Major's non-affair had been no more than gossip, so implausible that no proper paper even hinted at it. Every newspaper lawyer pointed out that denial was no defence against the dissemination of a libel. The law was doing a good job for Mr Major. He needed no writ.

The news of the writ gave the rumour a new status. It proved that gossip had drawn blood, the blood of the highest in the land. That in itself was a story and one which, under the rules of court, newspapers were permitted to carry. Besides, as every editor said to himself, how many libel writs in the past have been less than the truth and nothing but the truth? Many are bare-faced lies, issued only to suppress the truth. Writs are two-edged swords. They can either assert the truth against a lie or they can be a smokescreen behind which a victim gathers troops and prepares the next move. A newspaper may have no way of knowing which. Reporters are assigned to the story as a precaution. The walls of the Law Courts still echo to the perjuries of frightened politicians. I have received gagging writs on behalf of the most distinguished people. My reaction has always been, 'Oh dear, and

I thought he was innocent.' A writ may initially stop gossip from appearing in print, as did that issued by the Liberal leader, Paddy Ashdown, in 1990 over his affair with a former secretary. But it gives gossip the most almighty shot of adrenalin. In Mr Ashdown's case the gossip was later admitted to be true.

British public figures are highly sensitive on matters of sexual and financial probity. Some of them take the view, and others agree, that the only matters on which they are entitled to lie are sex and money. The one requirement is that they are not caught. If they are caught they must resign, however trivial the sin. The result gives newspapers inordinate power. Ministers and others performing public duties do so within accepted boundaries of incompetence. They can talk arrant nonsense about their jobs. They can throw thousands out of work. They can misallocate public money and jeopardize national security. In each case it is assumed that they mean well and do their best. They only resign when the Prime Minister tires of their face, which is not often. So their public misdemeanours merit scant investigation.

Yet most of them resign on the spot if the press discloses something amiss in their private lives. As a result, the invitation to delve could hardly be more enticing. The press knows that it cannot draw blood by scrutinizing the work of the executive, only by scrutinizing its play. The executive accepts the discipline. D. H. Lawrence was surely right. When the English peer into the more exotic reaches of human emotion, they become a 'snivelling, dribbling, dithering, palsied, pulse-less lot.' When it comes to the private behaviour of public figures, they deplore the executioner but excuse the execution. They shrug and ask for more.

There is nothing new in the penny dreadful persecution of famous people. Trollope built an entire novel, *Phineas Finn*, round the salacious antics of the journalist Quintus Slide. In Washington, Bill Clinton has been able to weather stories about his private life because it was inconceivable that he would resign over them. The more the president ignores or denies the stories, the more tedious and partisan they become. The private lives of public people rarely gleam in the full light of day. They abuse their spouses. They chastise or neglect their children. They are cruel to their aged parents. They fail to pay their bills on time. They are normal. But when I go into the polling booth I am trying to decide who will be a competent politician, not a competent spouse. We have enough trouble holding politicians to their public promises, without demanding they account for their private ones as well.

Editors, publicity agents and other moralists of church and state have long concocted an argument that 'if he cannot be trusted by his wife, how can he be trusted by the nation?' They used to concoct similar pseudo-concerns on the basis of possible KGB blackmail. Greater ingenuity is now required. The hounding from office of the arts minister, David Mellor, was justified on the grounds that his extramarital affair left him a poor speaker. The peeping Toms at Highgrove and the Princess of Wales's gymnasium excused themselves on the basis that they were showing how easy it would be to stage a telescopic lens assassination. The reprinting of transcripts of royal phone calls were meant to show 'the weakness of royal electronic security'. It is all humbug.

I believe John Major should not have sued and Sir Peter should not have resigned. By suing, the Prime Minister projected a story into every home in the land and encouraged the press to look for more. By resigning, Sir Peter accepted that there is no boundary between merit at work and merit in private life. He appeared to concede that the tabloid press, rather than his superiors, are the best judges of his fitness for office. By caving in to press intrusion, he invited further intrusion and gave the press a licence to reward those with 'information to offer'.

The resignation of the Chief of the Defence Staff shows that huge sums can be made by those who wish to kiss-and-tell and who can rely on the victim being driven from office by a sufficient hue and cry. Tabloid newspapers, in Sir Bernard Ingham's phrase, may be the sewers, but their informants and their victims are the sewage. Nothing opens the sluice

111

gates so wide as the readiness of victims to resign under pressure. The simplest antidote to all this is for public figures not to resign – or to sue – over disclosures that have no sensible relevance to their public duties. Above all they should disregard all disclosures that are to do with sex. In his much-misquoted aside, the Duke of Wellington is alleged to have told Harriet Walters, 'Publish and be damned!' when she warned he would be mentioned in her memoirs. But this richest of all *grandes horizontales* would never have stooped so low as to blackmail her most distinguished client. The Duke's phrase was actually written across a blackmail letter not from Walters but from her publisher, who held her memoirs and was desperate for money.

The dismissive reply was perhaps easier for the Duke than for a humble politician. But the principle is the same. The market for salacious gossip will only decline if the victim refuses to resign and the newspapers cease to pay. There is, wrote Chesterton, 'a terrible Circean law that if the soul stoops too ostentatiously to examine anything, it never gets up again.' He pointed out that in former times 'the educated class ignored the ruck of vulgar literature', including when it was itself the victim. Had Sir Peter not resigned, he would have found work tough for a while. He would have had to endure the sniggers of subordinates and the attention of the cameramen. That would have been the price of his foolishness. But his foolishness had no bearing on his public duties. He had a job for which, we assume, he was the best man. By resigning over an irrelevance he demeaned the job and the judgment of those who appointed him.

He also upped the price for kiss-and-tell scandals. The world watched spellbound. Who would be the next unfortunate Briton to be dragged through the town by the mob and stoned outside the city gates?

14

THE SCHOOL OF THE FUTURE

THE BURSAR gazed grim-faced down the table. 'Welcome,' he said quickly. The task was normally performed by the headmaster but he had deferred to the bursar on this occasion. 'I have called this emergency meeting of governors because you should know that St Cuthbert's faces a crisis. I need approval for drastic action.' He cleared his throat.

'Last summer the hayfever suffered by our three best A-level prospects meant that they achieved only E grades. This caused a 1.6 per cent drop in our league table score. Such is the quirkiness of the table that this decline led to a 120-place plunge in our ranking. I am sorry to say that we are now even lower than St Egbert's, a point I shall come to in a minute.

'The impact has been far worse than expected. Ten of our best pupils have said they intend to switch to other sixth forms within the year. This will devastate next year's score and ranking. There have been 30 new boy cancellations already. Applications are 30 per cent down. This is similar to the experience of other public schools that did poorly in the table. Many face ruin.'

A cloud of apprehension settled over the Old Library. The bursar went on, 'I must tell governors that as long as league tables are published in this crude form St Cuthbert's faces a vicious circle of decline. We may hope this lunacy does not last. For the time being we must fight or die. I propose that we fight, as Cuthbertians have done for over a century.

'This school has always been what we like to call well-rounded. The headmaster calls it a good comprehensive education for the middle classes of the county. I have asked him to stop using any of those sadly incorrect phrases. We have always got our brightest pupils into good universities and we have a coveted reputation in music, art and sport. We have also prided ourselves on our share of eccentrics, if I may quote the headmaster again, to leaven the scholastic loaf. These were mostly the offspring of old boys. We have also been lenient to our more wayward overseas pupils whose parents were so generous to the centenary appeal. We scoffed last year when St Egbert's expelled six potential E-graders for smoking.

'I tell the governors, we must scoff no more. That single act drove St Egbert's up 200 places in the league table. Our spies tell us that their applications are already 20 per cent up on last year. We simply cannot sit still or we shall have no pupils at all. St Cuthbert's must change. We must stop seeing new boys as smooth clay eager for the imprint of the Cuthbertian message. We must adopt a new motto, *per ardua ad pecuniam*. Our output is a function of our inputs, and we must look to them with greater care.

'The government has laid down that we shall be judged in public on our A-level performance alone. So be it. This must become our sole objective. Nor must we fool ourselves about our ability to add value by our excellent teaching. The fact is that if we select duds at 13 we shall get duds at 16, and if we keep those duds into the sixth form we are doomed. There must be no more duds.'

The bursar paused, with an excessive sense of theatre. He threw a glance at the headmaster, who was shrinking into the chair beside him. 'The headmaster and I have set ourselves the challenge of raising St Cuthbert's league ranking by 250 places over the next two years. We simply must be in the

John Patten top 50. Mr McKintosh in the maths department has calculated that the ranking margins are so small that this requires no more than a four point rise in our A-level average per candidate. But we cannot rely on a low pollen count to deliver this. I therefore ask for the governors' support for a series of urgent measures. They are not for the squeamish, but they are firmly in line with government policy. Everything I am about to propose is at present being implemented or seriously considered by other English public schools.

'First to stop the rot we must act directly on next year's figures. This means getting rid of the dross. We have marked at least 30 sixth formers said by their form masters to be unlikely A- or B-graders. We want them out. House masters have been told to see them expelled by hook or crook, preferably in the exam term to maximize fee income in the interim. Short of planting drugs in their tuck boxes, we shall act on the slightest misdemeanour.

'Alongside this we must head-hunt. Two senior masters have been appointed talent scouts. One of them, Mr Snodgrass, did similar work many years ago when the rugger team was in the doldrums and old boys were complaining that St Cuthbert's was "not the school it was". We survived that threat. I understand an agency is already offering a computerized data base of 13- and 14-year-olds with A- and B-grade potential and currently in low ranking schools. I imagine a number of our boys are on this list.

'Buying this data base will be expensive. Buying the pupils will be even more so. When Cranbourne Chase closed in 1992, I saw jackals picking over that corpse for potential A/ Bs. There was much talk of free places offered and even of commissions being paid for names and addresses. There will be other closures soon. The headmaster must be there with the pack, chequebook in hand.

'Governors will understand that parents of bright children are aware of this situation. They are mercenary. They know a marketable product when they have one. Already 12- and 13-year-olds with A/B potential are being peddled from school to school by their parents like superbrat film stars.

115

They refuse to sit our entrance exam and expect us to accept them on the say-so of a prep school headmaster, a breed not unacquainted with corruption. Children are then auctioned for fee discounts without a mention of sitting the scholarship.

'We shall have the devil of a job sorting out the quality inputs from the con artists. But they are all using the league tables as leverage. I know of schools that have been told to their faces, "We were hoping for a better offer", and "Don't call us, we'll call you." I have even had an Old Cuthbertian demanding a 30 per cent discount for an odious child he called a "gilt-edged A/B cert"! None the less I have agreed to give the headmaster discretion to negotiate fees on the spot.

'As a result, we may be forced to recoup some of this lost income by making our fees variable according to performance up the school. If a child pre-sold as a mini-Einstein turns out to be a fraud, we shall have to introduce some quality control. We intend to hold internal exams each term for every boy in the school. The results will be computerized and converted into a termly fee invoice to parents. We must watch our cash flow here. We do not want to find our sixth form composed one hundred per cent of discounts. We have, however, set aside a "Top 50 investment fund" to meet the current target. This means gambling on a heavy overdraft next year in the hope of bringing in extra fee payers the year after.

'I now come to a matter of some sensitivity. I am sure parents will take the view that if fees are to be performance-linked, so should teachers' pay. We must agree. As of this term, I am putting all fifth and sixth form teachers onto per-formance-related contracts. Remuneration will be based quite simply on the exam results of boys in their charge. There will be bonuses for any A/B prospects they can entice from other schools. We have discussed this with the staff. They have pleaded that their extra-curricular work, such as sport and tuition for less able boys, be included in their pay package. This is out of the question. The league tables recognize no such work. Nor can we. This is a cruel world, a return to Victorian payment by results. The strain on staff may be intense and governors should expect some pupils to disappear

116

in suspicious circumstances. We must take this in our stride.'

The governors were by now ashen. The bishop had a choking fit. Portraits of Old Cuthbertians looked down grimly from the library walls. Books seemed to quake in their jackets. But the bursar was not finished. Worse was to come.

'Every school in Britain is now being measured against every other. The league tables are a nationalization of standards. St Cuthbert's must abandon its attachment, which I fear we must treat as nostalgic, to our catchment area, to the county and to the children of old boys. Such sentiment must be anathema. In particular we must be vigilant against local prep schools polluting our results with potential D- and E-graders. There may be a case for introducing a special non-exam stream for foreign pupils. We have used a fruitful agency in Hong Kong and are discussing with our lawyers whether we can secure overseas fee income without having to declare the pupils for exam result purposes.

'The headmaster and I have set up a committee to examine the practice already known in other schools as "grade stripping". We already counsel prospective D/E-graders to leave early in their own best interest, to avoid them contaminating the A-level figures. We are considering housing the duller sixth formers on full fees in a separate boarding house offering the full St Cuthbert's facilities but under a distinct identity. We are provisionally calling this St Cuthbert's School of Technology. It would make a separate A-level return. This may require a new holding company and subsidiary board structure. I shall keep the finance committee informed. This might also be a way of transforming our ranking overnight.'

The bursar's audience was by now stunned. He felt his ascendancy grow while the headmaster sat shrivelled by his side. He decided on one last turn of the screw. 'Many sixth forms above us in the league table are little more than exam factories and crammers. Indeed there were two crammers in the 1993 top twenty. They sweat pupils and they sweat themselves. Only their ranking keeps them in being. We at St Cuthbert's have always despised such forcing-houses. Our friends in universities and industry have acknowledged that

a well-rounded Cuthbertian is more use than a force-fed one.
But those days are gone. The league tables ignore such qualities. I have regretfully accepted the resignations of the music
and art staff.

'The world is for the smart. Big schools will get bigger and
richer. Lesser schools will simply fail. St Cuthbert's cannot
afford to be second best. Nowadays it is sink or cram. As a
gesture of our collective commitment to cramming, I have
proposed to the headmaster that all sport at St Cuthbert's
will be confined to the hobby hour. We anticipate that
this will save the salaries of our two physical education
teachers. The market place does not judge us on the rugby
field. Those boys who want exercise can go to the local rec-
reation ground after school. I propose to reseed the cricket
pitch with rape or lucerne and put it forward to Brussels next
year for a set-aside grant.'

The bursar was done. Behind his back, an old and tarnished
challenge cup, won in days of Cuthbertian greatness, tilted
slowly on its shelf and fell to the ground with a crash.
Nobody moved. Nobody dared.

15

OLYMPUS MANCUNIENSIS

THE AMERICAN looked at me with a puzzled smile. 'Manchester? You can't be serious?' Deadly serious, I said, and deadly depressed. Britain had just been told that Sydney was to host the Olympic Games in the year 2000. Manchester had lost. And we had been so sure it would win. This was a blow to national pride, but the shock for me was even greater for having this polite American couple tell me to my face that they had assumed Manchester was joking. 'Manchester is Dickens, and smoke, and rain,' they said with a laugh, 'everything that is decrepit and out of date. Sydney is modern and sunny and young and has that marvellous harbour and opera house.' Surely I was having them on. Manchester's bid had that much-valued quality in British humour, a sense of irony.

I fell silent. Perhaps we had all been victims of chauvinist political correctness. We had deluded ourselves. Manchester had never been in with a chance. As Bob Payton, the American entrepreneur, remarked when asked what had gone wrong, 'I knew you would lose from the moment I saw the salesman's ties.' They were striped with monogram motifs and worn with blazers. Their wearers looked like a pale-faced 1960s British athletics team in mufti. Sydney's bronzed beauties had wiped the floor with the Olympics committee.

A rose by any other name might smell as sweet, but no amount of cologne could make Manchester smell of anything but Manchester.

I admired Manchester's bid for its shamelessness. This had nothing to do with the chippy, inverted snobbery of London Mancunians. Nor did I admire the manner in which London politicians and media backed the bid as a patronizing gesture to the hopeless North. I liked the gall with which Manchester presented itself as the virile modern metropolis of the twenty-first century. This was not *Hard Times* on the running track. The salesmen struggled to present Manchester as a modern city ideally adjusted to the synthetic commercialism of the Olympics. This at least was the spirit that made Manchester what it once had been. It was a desperate grasp at renaissance.

By all accounts, the bid was technically faultless. Athletes would have been sumptuously housed, effortlessly transported, accelerated to stardom with all the proficiency of modern technology. An estimated £200m was being spent on 'infrastructure', an indefinite amount of this to be of permanent use. £75m came from central government funds. The public relations was superb, the best £5m could buy. Bob Scott, the organizer, became a Mancunian hero. John Major and the Princess Royal added *gravitas* to the video-tape hyperbole of the final voting in Monte Carlo. When Britain lost, they did the traditional stiff upper lip act. The only thing nobler than a Briton in victory is a Briton in defeat. Mr Scott was declared Sir Robert. Had he won I bet he would still be plain Mr.

Yet every streetwise Olympic pundit was saying the same from the start. Only two cities are ever likely to win the Olympics for Britain. They are London and Edinburgh. London was not in the running. Central government now runs London and the last thing central government is capable of handling is an Olympics bid. With the local boroughs at each other's throats, the lack of any political basis for a bid would make co-operation on sites and facilities impossible. Edinburgh was in Scotland and was run in the 1980s by a far left council. It had coped, none too successfully, with a

Commonwealth games. It did not want to bid. Manchester was thus the best hope. For the government it offered a least worst solution. There was no risk of the bid succeeding, yet the government could appear to be supporting the North by giving it a 'leg up'.

Any European bid for the Olympics had to have a positive image, if only because Europe had hosted the last Olympics at Barcelona. America was hosting the next and Africa, Asia or Australasia were bound to have a greater chance of success after that. Image was all. Any number of velodromes, mono-rails, Olympic villages and fun-packed videos would be money down the drain if the name of the city did not itself sound exciting. Not even an Einstein of public relations could do that to Manchester. The name was redolent of ugly industrial past.

I believe that the failure of Manchester's bid was the nemesis of everything that Britain has done to its great cities for the past half century. The Manchester of Dickens, Engels and Free Trade was black in its chimneys, black in its commercial houses, black in its brick and stone. Manchester's image was tough and hard. It was unredeemed by the scenic drama of Liverpool or Glasgow or Newcastle. Even Birmingham had managed to project itself as a city reborn to the modern age. Manchester had found no such wellspring of renewal. What tore its bid apart was not the fact of its industrial past or of wartime destruction. Olympic Munich had an industrial past and suffered horrendous wartime bombing. So had Seoul. Barcelona and Mexico City had grim pasts, and much that is grim about their present environment. What ruined Manchester was its inability to pull itself out of the past, or at least the methods by which it tried.

In the 1960s and 70s, government housing policy and a left-wing local council literally wrecked much of Manchester. Together they destroyed more of the standing fabric of the city than was destroyed probably in any other city in the free world. When Pevsner visited Manchester in 1969 he remarked that he had 'walked through areas of total desolation'.

Making a film there in the 1970s I remember visiting advice

centres for the tens of thousands of inhabitants being
'decanted' into out-of-town estates. They were being
removed compulsorily from communities they had occupied
as united families since the nineteenth century, communities
in which they had survived two world wars. They were like
dazed refugees, wondering what was happening to them. I
spoke to a Polish resident who told me it was indeed 'like
the war all over again'. They had to watch as bulldozers
flattened perfectly good homes, all to the service of modern
architecture and town planning. The result is modern Salford,
Hulme and Moss Side, a townscape of bleak high-rises and
no-go areas, vats of tribulation into which every social poison
is stirred and made more lethal.

Manchester's municipal leadership was never able to
respond to economic decline by asking what young and enterprising Mancunians were after. They offered them nowhere
to live or work and let them drift south to London. Instead,
huge sums were spent on cheap system-built housing, adorning the city's inner suburbs with the drabness of Eastern
Europe. Curtain walls and concrete boxes punctuated every
street and loomed over every vacant lot. Most obtrusive was
the 1960 Piccadilly Hotel, lying slovenly alongside Piccadilly
Gardens in the city centre. That was how Manchester lost its
Olympics bid. No amount of shepherding and razzmatazz
could shield visiting members of the International Olympic
Committee from these sights. They were the city red in tooth,
claw and politics.

Manchester in its prime was a true Second City of the
nation. From the Gothic gables of Waterhouse's town hall to
the swirling strings of the Hallé Orchestra; from the *palazzi*
of Ancoats to cosy medieval Chetham's; from the roar of Old
Trafford to the high-minded lectures of the Free Trade Hall,
this was a noble republic. Carlyle found Manchester 'every
whit as wonderful, as fearful, as unimaginable as the oldest
Salem'. To Disraeli, who had come to detest the appearance
of Georgian London, Manchester was 'the most wonderful
city of modern times'. The streets that this Manchester left
to the twentieth century were black only with surface soot.

122

Underneath they were bright red and white, grey, ochre and coffee. The city's Victorian architecture was brilliant. Its buildings took their stylistic cue from Renaissance Florence, Siena and Rome, capitals of medieval commerce. Manchester was one of the great creations of nineteenth-century Europe. Thirty years ago, the city was more or less intact. A wash down, a lick of paint and some improvement to its street furniture and Manchester could have stood as proud on the Olympic stage as any Barcelona.

In the 1970s and 80s, Manchester's Labour leadership decided not to follow in the footsteps of Westminster, Glasgow and Bristol and acknowledge the mistakes of the recent past. It rejected conservation as the guiding spirit of its renewal and followed Liverpool into the dark tunnel of anti-capitalist *dirigisme*. The ethos of free trade was supplanted by union protectionism, private regeneration by public redevelopment, conservation by slash and build. Visiting Manchester in those years, I felt I was indeed drifting back to *Hard Times*. Councillors still seemed determined to avenge Stephen Blackpool's death. They still believed socialism could redeem the sins of Manchester's capitalist record: 'Who could look on 't, Sir, and fairly tell a man 'tis not a muddle?' Planning and public expenditure would sort out the muddle.

Today's socialist city is no less a muddle. Victorian *palazzi* have either been demolished or left to rot. Individual works survive in the central streets like odd teeth. The route from Whitworth Street to Ancoats along the Rochdale Canal corridor might have formed a linear conservation area that would be humming with life in any equivalent German or North American city. It would have taken pride of place in an Olympics brochure. Other countries can see the economic potential of restored old districts. The best conservation Manchester could achieve by the early 1990s was the Castlefields canal basin and a small Chinatown. There are fine buildings, the Town Hall, the University, the Rylands Library, Chetham's. But they seem adrift in a city that has given up on its appearance. Manchester lacks a topographical feature to give it visual coherence, like Liverpool's river front and

Newcastle's hill. It made up for this in the bravura of its street architecture. Yet civic leaders regard this architecture as a capitalist symbol that should be eliminated.

American 'rust-belt' cities investigating their post-industrial salvation have come up with surprising answers. New investors claim initially that what they want of a city is infrastructure, motorways, access to markets, good factories and a well-trained labour force. Further enquiry shows that they want no such things. Consultants have discovered that the crucial factor in locational decisions is a city's image. How do senior executives and their wives react to the mention of a city's name? Cities in the American north-east and mid-west have found that young, mobile workers, including existing residents wondering whether to move elsewhere, seek originality and excitement. They want something with 'buzz' that they can boast about to friends and relatives. They value not economic infrastructure but intangible 'civic' qualities. To be more specific, say the consultants, these people want to experience a respect for history, good universities, quaint neighbourhoods, art galleries, symphony orchestras, 'people draws' – what in marketing jargon is called niche excellence.

The Olympic city that offered just this mix of qualities was Sydney. People who had never been there identified it with two physical objects and one climatic phenomenon: a nineteenth-century bridge, a twentieth-century opera house and constant sun. Sydney Opera House was regarded as an extravagant white elephant in its day. Yet it was the star of the city's Olympics bid. As such that building must be the most lucrative single investment the city ever made in its post-industrial future. The opera house profile loomed over its bid. Nor was Sydney the first to appreciate the role that history and environment play in creating an urban image. Other Olympic cities had done the same. Rome promoted its past greatness. Barcelona promoted its medieval core. Los Angeles drew on its entertainment heritage. Manchester tried to promote the warmth of its people. Britons may know them to be warm. But the nearest most outsiders get to Mancunians is *Coronation Street*. And *Coronation Street* has none of the youthful freshness of *Neighbours*.

Can Manchester be saved? It must be the hardest nut for any urban renewer to crack. There is little chance of the place being able to correct fully the mistakes of post-war redevelopment. The scale of the necessary demolition and rebuilding would be enormous. There can be piecemeal improvement. Manchester is a popular university centre and efforts are being made to move students into high-rise blocks no longer considered habitable by families or old people. The fragmentary conservation areas in the centre and Salford docks might have new life blown into them. But this is unlikely to overcome the 'image trauma' experienced by most visitors. Inward investors and outward migrants will continue to seek the office parks of Cheshire or telecommute from the villages in the adjacent Pennines.

Manchester could go for broke on what it still has: restoring its surviving old buildings and infilling where possible with good new ones. It could push the Hallé orchestra back into the top class, build a new opera house and a Tate-of-the-North blatantly to rival Liverpool's. It has an excellent science museum and lively theatre at the Royal Exchange. The lesson of American experience is that these must be made incontrovertibly the best in the land if Manchester is to draw strength from their presence. That in turn requires the city to acknowledge the part that the arts and conservation play in promoting its external image.

The Olympics bid brought a remarkable unity of purpose to Manchester's leadership. A city long wracked with political discord did rediscover some of its own municipal pride. I believe that pride will have little meaning unless it is allied to a revived local democracy. And that in turn means returning to cities some discretion over local taxation and expenditure. The present government is most unlikely to permit this. Cities are run locally but with resources and priorities fixed centrally in Whitehall or through quangos appointed by Whitehall. I was amused to see one government minister after another lining up to back Manchester's bid.

125

They were ready to take full credit should a miracle occur and Manchester win. But when the party was over, Manchester returned below the political salt. It stays there.

16

THE DEATH OF
ECONOMIC MAN

THE INDIAN government has been ridiculed for consulting astrologers before making important economic decisions. In reply a spokesman points out that Indian rulers have always done so and anyway, what is the harm? Some leading British companies retain, or used to retain, the services of horoscope writers. Nancy Reagan consulted soothsayers. Come to that, the British cabinet is up to the same trick. It has been hiring economic forecasters. The Chancellor of the Exchequer has gone one better. He has appointed not one forecaster – thus achieving unanimity – but many. 'Seven Wise Men' gather each four months to examine the entrails of the sacred geese and give their verdict. Seven was always a magic number. It should yield a voting majority, though in the world of economists, who can say?

I sometimes wonder what profession will one day be regarded with derision, as most of us might regard astrologers or wart-charmers. In 1976 the London Met Office stopped publishing what were called long-range weather forecasts, looking forward months into the future. The reason was simple. They were so conjectural as to be worthless. Even the biggest computer could not encompass the variables required to makes its judgments better than random. It yielded a range of options so wide as to be of no predictive value to the man in the street. I thought this intellectual humility stood much to the Met Office's credit.

Macro-economic forecasters fall into the same category. Governments, banks and commercial organizations like to have one or two in their retinue, like medieval friars. They ward off the evil eye. I remember being on the board of a large company whose in-house economist would attend quarterly meetings and give his verdict on the state of the economy and his vision for its future. We listened reverentially. What we heard never differed from what we read in newspapers. Yet we felt more comfortable having the chap on call. We never took the slightest notice of a word he said.

I am careful here to distinguish macro-economists from the micro variety. My villains are the former, who purport to study national aggregates and especially those who predict their likely movement in response to various stimuli. Micro-economists confine their enthusiasm to the behaviour of individuals and firms, usually relying on more exact statistics and more limited relationships. In economics as in all things, I find small is beautiful.

The start of the 1990s saw macro-economists take a fearful drubbing. Their worst period was after Britain left the European exchange rate mechanism and devalued the pound on 'Black Wednesday' in September 1992. Before this climactic event, the Treasury and its political boss, Norman Lamont, were adamant that leaving the mechanism would not, could not, mean lower interest rates. Indeed it might well mean higher ones. 'The illusion that devaluation would enable us to make a substantial reduction in interest rates', said Mr Lamont to the *Financial Times*, 'is fool's gold.' The *Financial Times* agreed with him. So did the august *Economist*, along with Whitehall's economic establishment and the Bank of England. The rest of Fleet Street (including *The Times*) was more sceptical. But government economists were adamant that Britain needed the discipline of the European monetary system if market confidence was to be maintained and interest rates fall.

Within six months of Britain leaving the mechanism, interest rates had tumbled to half of what they had been at the moment of departure. They did precisely the opposite of what the experts had said they would do. There were, I am sure, other factors at play. The briefing given to ministers and the press may have been immaculate in its subordinate clauses and qualifications. But I remember it well. We were left in no doubt that the horrors of life outside the ERM were such as to make lower interest rates at that stage inconceivable. Macro-economists have a nasty habit of looking you in the eye and saying things so unpalatable as to unnerve even the most committed sceptic. Like Savonarola, they will wag their finger and warn of dire consequences if their advice is not followed. If things go wrong, they can claim to have been right. If things turn out better than predicted, most people will forget that the economists were ever wrong.

The interaction of the components of a modern economy is a subject that most people can comprehend only in short bursts with ice-packs on their heads. Time was when economics kept its public prescriptions simple. The nation was told to concentrate on one thing and prosperity would be round the corner, be it the balance of payments, the sterling exchange rate, the public sector borrowing requirement or the inflation rate. We forgot that the lodestar changed each few years. But at least there was a lodestar.

Now all is confusion. Economists leap into print unsure whether interest rates should go up or down, or whether they *will* go up or down if particular policies are chosen. Students are faced with a searing intellectual cocktail: the pound is falling, unemployment is rising, the balance of payments is deteriorating, public borrowing is too high, taxation is too low, the government must act. The economist is like a pre-Newtonian physicist, waiting in painful anticipation for an apple to fall. Yet he pushes on with his advice. One minute he explains that there is absolutely no alternative to fighting inflation with a fixed price for sterling, high interest rates and a shrinking public sector. The next he turns turtle. A floating pound, low interest rates and an expanding public sector is apparently fine and indeed need not lead to rising inflation. This nonsense is then fed into the mouths of politicians and leader writers, where it is regurgitated in even more garbled form.

The era of the economist is, I believe, drawing to a close. Politicians and officials alike are pointing at them and declaring them naked. Economics derived its status from the era of 'can-do' politics. Government believed that nothing could be beyond its remit. All markets were better if regulated. All prices were better if fixed. Speculators were the incarnation of evil. Only get the aggregates right, only garner enough statistics, and something called 'economic policy' would see you safely on the road to stable growth. Those who see the state as an ordered system will accord power to those who claim to understand it.

Economic forecasters were the light cavalry of this power. Their computerized statistics glinted in the political sun. The nation's chief economic adviser, Sir Terry Burns, took over in 1991 as head of the Treasury. He professed scepticism about forecasting. In a 1986 paper to the Royal Society of Arts, he pointed out that forecasting was a phenomenal growth industry: from two computer models in the 1960s to over 30 in the 1980s. Yet, he admitted, there had been 'no marked improvement in Treasury forecasts of output and inflation up to a forecasting horizon of about a year' over the entire period. Only in the long term did he expect to see things improve. This was before the horrors of the 'no recession' forecasts which blighted Government policy in the late-Eighties as it drifted into the longest post-war recession. Yet the forecasts continued to appear.

For Sir Terry and his predecessors, membership of the European exchange rate club was a central article of faith. They were brusque to any outsiders who questioned whether this was good for prosperity in Britain or whether, without the ERM, Britain might have endured a less severe recession and an earlier recovery. I believe they were not just wrong. By September 1992 they had become massively and catastrophically wrong, and were proved to be so by subsequent events. Thousands of businesses, hundreds of thousands of people, were ruined by bankruptcy and unemployment. The years 1990 to 1992 were the Treasury's Dardanelles campaign. Sitting most days on the sofas of the Reform Club in London are the men who played a part in this shambles. No Treasury or Bank of England resignations followed Black Wednesday. If economics had been a true profession rather than an academic 'discipline', hearings would have been heard and individuals struck off. I have seen no post mortems of the economic reasoning of the 1992 U-turn, despite exhaustive reconstructions of the political events at the time. (Pollsters conducted a public enquiry into their own 1992 general election débâcle, but they are paid per poll and had reputations to repair.) The Treasury silence was broken only by the noise of forecasters cashing pay cheques.

Like the climatologist, the economist can wander the fields of history and trace the general pattern of events. Economic history is an exciting endeavour and a guide to political wisdom. But like the climatologist, the economist lacks the essence of a true science, the ability to make verifiable forecasts. He can offer no more than intelligent guesses on the basis of past experience. Denis Healey, one of the Treasury's more spirited incumbents, warned in his autobiography against treating economics as anything approaching a science. He regarded it as social psychology. He vowed to make economic forecasters 'distrusted for ever' for their persistent extrapolations from 'a partially known past, through an unknown present to an unknowable future'. He might recall the intellectual anguish of the econometrician who told his wife he loved her very much. 'Exactly how much is that?' she retorted.

I suppose it is in the nature of a novice profession to oversell itself and erect a stockade of jargon to protect its mysteries from outsiders. Art historians are the same. Forecasting must be politically credible, since politicians are the forecaster's principal clients. Yet the adviser must be careful to cover himself against failure. He uses such phrases as 'other things being equal' or 'international conditions permitting'.

Bad outcomes must be blamed on advice not being precisely followed. Sometimes this will be a fair excuse. But macro-economics – the economics of national wealth – is an accessory to the fact of political crime. It peddles bogus objectivity at which desperate ministers can grasp. Statistics purporting to measure unemployment or money supply or retail price movements, as Sir Terry has admitted, are extremely hard to measure. So hard, he did not care to ask, as not to be worth measuring at all?

Push an economist against the wall and he will admit that international comparisons of unemployment or domestic product are next to meaningless. He will agree that 'manufacturing industry' is no longer a useful economic concept. Yet he will continue to pretend otherwise. He will make forecasts on demand. If the client is offering good money to know his fortune, what harm is there in mumbling about the cusp of Aquarius and Pisces? As Marshall wrote in 1919: 'The chief purpose of every study of human action should be to suggest the probable outcome of present tendencies; thus to indicate, tacitly if not expressly, such modifications of those tendencies as might further the well-being of mankind.' Note the phrase, tacitly if not expressly! This might do as the forecaster's Hippocratic Oath.

One of the few economists lately to have called this bluff is Professor Paul Ormerod. He did so first at the 1992 British Association conference, when he pilloried the modelling and forecasting errors that underpinned policy during the recession then current. They were, he said, worse than useless, since ministers were deliberately choosing economists likely to support their own views. Ormerod, who had himself been head of the Henley Forecasting Centre, went on to accuse macro-economics of being 'littered with new concepts which have given little insight into how economies actually work'. Instead it had been seduced into forecasting and was now in disarray. 'The forecasting record of the models', he said, 'was never brilliant and has deteriorated since the mid-1980s; in virtually every Western country serious errors have been made.' Ormerod quoted one American survey of prominent forecasters which discovered that almost all fared worse than the prediction: 'Things will go on more or less as they did last year.' He concluded that most macro-economic modelling should be 'abandoned or at least suspended until it can find a sounder empirical base'.

The professor went on from these strictures to commit professional genocide. In his book, *The Death of Economics*, he catalogued the forecasting failures of economists in 1993 alone. They had failed to predict, and therefore failed to prepare policy-makers for, the Japanese recession, the American recovery, the collapse of the German economy and the turmoil of the ERM following Britain's withdrawal. As for the 'soft landing' that was confidently forecast for the end of the 1980s boom, the less said the better. A more humble, or perhaps less paranoid, profession might have shut up shop and gone fishing.

The Treasury's response is to cling to the qualifications in Sir Terry Burns's 1986 lecture and point out that it is the only forecaster regularly to publish data on its own accuracy. In a paper published in June 1991 it admitted that things went badly wrong in the late 1980s when there were 'large differences between most forecasts and outturn'. These were apparently 'due in part to problems with the quality of economic statistics' and to 'unprecedented changes in private sector activity'. Needless to say, the Treasury would like more, not fewer, statisticians to improve the quality of the figures – an endearing conceit. Newspapers are still full of what look suspiciously like forecasts, usually in a constant state of being 'revised up or down'. If there is anything remotely like good news lurking over the horizon, a politician will naturally grasp at it, even as he declares his total disbelief in its validity. I am sure the Indian government takes the same view of its astrology.

Is there anything to put in place of this scepticism? Economies exist, money circulates, exchange rates move, people find jobs and lose them, governments raise and lower taxes. Are there no rules to guide those whose decisions influence these phenomena? What Ormerod does is articulate in

133

layman's language the intellectual limitations of conventional economics. He seems to me to clear the ground of weeds, the better to see what flowers can eventually grow. Most economic phenomena, he points out, are simply not quantifiable. One man's leisure hour is spent enjoyably sleeping in his garden, another's is spent furiously injecting money into the economy by driving, eating out, buying clothes and theatre tickets. These two patterns of behaviour may yield an identical personal benefit, yet they will have a different impact on any calculation of the gross domestic product. Likewise, unemployment criteria are changed almost every year, not just to keep statisticians in business but because the concept itself is so fluid. The boundaries between economic categories are always grey. As Nigel Lawson complained in his apologia for the 1987–88 boom, the measurement of personal credit altered completely at the time with the growth of building society accounts. People would keep doing things without asking the economists' permission!

The mathematics of uncertainty is only beginning to make an impact on what are wrongly termed the social sciences. Paul Gleick, in his recent book *Chaos*, mentioned that the movement of money in an economy is not unlike the movement of air currents over the earth's surface. There is some long-term order in the chaos. Low pressure areas tend to gather off Iceland and high pressure ones over the Azores. But in the short term all is uncertainty. The fluttering of a butterfly's wing can divert a tiny airstream, which deflects a bigger one, which deflects a storm-cloud. A tiny deflection in mid-Atlantic brought the 1987 hurricane ashore in southern England when it had been predicted to stay over the sea. Likewise small shifts in taxation, in confidence, in foreign trade, in the weather or in fashion can divert an economy into unforeseeable patterns of spending and saving. Modern economies, as Mr Healey said, are unknowables. In the short term they are intellectually chaotic. It is in the short term that we all live.

To this extent, the construction of models to measure an economy is a fool's errand. The more complex I make the model, the closer I may believe I am getting to reality, and the more easily I may convince my client of this. But the opposite is true. The apparent certainties of such models are a snare and delusion. To be sure, economic phenomena are related to each other. My decision to spend rather than save influences the profits of the shop or the liquidity of the bank. But so interwoven are these relationships as to be indeterminate collectively or over time: they cannot be added up and assessed so that generalized conclusions can be drawn. Each decision impacts on every other. As the Greek philosophers noted, everything is in flux.

To Ormerod, the economic orthodoxies studied at university – the theory of competitive equilibrium, the theory of marginal utility, the theory of market clearing prices – are seductive nonsense. They describe ideal economic states. In real ones markets do not clear, prices do not equate demand and supply, individuals use money irrationally. By all means study these markets. By all means examine how individuals behave when spending or saving, how firms make decisions and governments choose priorities. But remember that you are studying psychological variables that are unsusceptible of empirical proof. Beware of mathematics. Always beware of prediction. The only true economics is history. And even history is blessed with as many theories as professorships.

17

LETHAL WEAPONS

WONDERS NEVER cease. The British actor Sir Anthony Hopkins has stated that he will not make a sequel to his Oscar-winning performance as a cannibal in the film, *Silence of the Lambs*. Explaining his decision he said that he had discovered that some children in Cardiff had seen the film, despite it being rated as unsuitable for those under 18. This had shocked him. 'There are such terrifying films coming that I think it may be time to say, enough is enough,' was his reported comment. He added, 'As an actor I do have to have some responsibility.' The offer for a *Silence of the Lambs Two* was believed to be over one million dollars.

I agree with Sir Anthony, but am no less shocked that *he* should have been shocked. Any 12-year-old of my acquaintance has complete access to his films, especially the 18-rated ones, from any video store. I am equally intrigued by the concept of actors having 'some responsibility' for the consequences of their work. I wonder if directors, writers, producers and backers feel the same. And do they extend this new-found sense of responsibility beyond children to adults? The debate on the impact of violent or sexually explicit entertainment on spectators is as old as Roman circuses. What is new is the double standard. Film-makers have long claimed cultural influence for their medium, rather like modern artists. The early American movie-makers were eager to establish themselves as above and beyond entertainment. According to Daniel Boorstin in his history of American culture, they claimed 'the power to be mistaken for reality . . . to make us walk more confidently on the precarious ground of the imagination'. The French director, Jean-Luc Godard agreed. He remarked that, 'Cinema is truth 24 times a second.' Costa-Gavras's works were lauded as revolutionary statements that helped topple Greek and Latin-American dictators. Nor is such grandiosity confined to political cinema. Woody Allen mournfully remarked, 'If I have made one more person feel miserable, then I'll feel I've done my job.'

The claim that cinema can induce predictable responses in its audience is shared by the courtiers to this art form. Advertisers believe plugs in movies can change spending habits. Charities use documentaries to raise money. Manufacturers feel it worth having stars endorse their products. Governments subsidize films to boost national prestige. I find it mystifying that if the moving image is regarded as so influential in these respects it should not be considered influential in its portrayal of sex, violence or political extremism. It is an insult to reason to claim that adults (or children) can be moved to one sort of action but not to another by a filmed image – least of all images so disturbing as those depicting rape, sadism, cruelty or sexual stimulation. Nor is this a matter of simple common sense. America is now awash in studies showing either a clear causal link between those exposed to screen violence and subsequent violent behaviour, or at least some anecdotal correlation between the two.

We prosecute those who encourage euthanasia or who incite racial hatred. We do so because we believe that these actions have consequences that outweigh the infringement of free speech. It strains credulity to believe that films portraying the depths of human depravity are harmless entertainment. Those producing them must have seriously deranged personalities if they think this. I would prefer them to say they are simply in it for the money. Some film-makers cope with the

137

paradox by scrambling their minds with jargon. The actor Michael Douglas has defended his ultra-violent film *Falling Down*, which was rejected by most studios as being too irresponsible – note the word 'too'. Douglas pointed out (in the *Daily Mail*) that the film 'is an original voice that really speaks for the moment . . . people struggling to deal with their lives while trying to make sense of a very illogical world'. Mr Douglas's contribution to making sense is to wander Los Angeles spraying anybody he meets with a machine-gun, especially anybody Korean. This had local audiences cheering the killer to the rafters. Mr Douglas might agree with the director of many violent films, Martin Scorsese, who suggested that 'maybe we need the catharsis of blood-letting and decapitation' from time to time.

If a politician or a judge said this, they would be treated as raving mad. What licence entitles the artist to spout such rubbish? The American critic Michael Medved has been reviled by many in Hollywood for commenting that these films cannot but encourage young and old Americans alike to the view that 'physical intimidation is irresistibly sexy and that violence offers an effective solution for all human problems'. But Medved has an increasing body of supporters. Long gone are the days when such violence needed to be shown as 'not paying in the end', when right triumphed. Even the comedy *The Player* showed its hero committing a particularly bloody murder on his way to personal and professional happiness.

Mr Medved has suggested that the public may at last be turning from these films. Producers and directors have always said they would love to produce *Gone with the Wind*, but it is the public who will not let them. Yet violent movies appear to be driving the public away from cinemas. A horrible film may beat a less horrible one within the market, but the market as a whole is contracting. Newcomers are less interested. Decent people do not want to see lumps bitten out of women's cheeks, corpses splattered over ceilings or genitalia slashed with razors. This sort of stuff is strictly for a dwindling group of addicts.

Some believe the film business is sliding away from public cinemas and towards a narrow semi-pornographic market for videos and cable television channels. This must make its dissemination ever more subject to the risk of censorship. Britain has taken measures to restrict the output, if not the manufacture, of sex and violence videos to which children might have access. The rating system is being tightened and the renting of videos to children placed on a par with alcohol. The courts are being given stricter powers over pornography. If the written word can be controlled, why not the filmed image? The pre-war American film, *Birth of a Nation*, was widely and plausibly credited with leading to the revival of the Ku-Klux Klan. Mr Douglas's new film has done nothing for American-Korean relations. If directors say commercial pressure forces them to ask actresses to remove their clothes on screen and simulate copulation, why should legal pressure not force them to desist? Let commercial censorship be replaced with legal censorship. As Mr Medved mildly points out, the age of sexual censorship coincided with some of Hollywood's greatest artistry, with films such as *Stagecoach*, *Of Mice and Men*, *Drums along the Mohawk* and *Wuthering Heights*.

Sex and violence are not the limits of the film business's current self-indulgence. When not out to deprave and corrupt it is seeking instead to confuse history with propaganda. I recently gasped, or sobbed, through three films that purport to tell a true story, and use that truth as part of their impact on the viewer. They are *Shadowlands*, *In the Name of the Father* and *Schindler's List*. They come hard on the heels of another of the genre, Oliver Stone's *JFK*, a film about the Kennedy assassination.

I approached *Shadowlands* with trepidation. Sir Richard Attenborough washes his films in tears much as Michael Winner washes his in blood. The film is a sumptuous evocation of post-war Oxford life as well as of mature love, that of C. S. Lewis and Joy Gresham. I thoroughly enjoyed it and wept at all the required moments. But the opening sequence was categorical: 'This is a true story.' It was not *based on* a

139

true story, or taken from a book of a true story, but claimed to be a real account of what actually happened to a group of people who lived in 1950s Oxford.

The film is no such thing. Andrew Wilson may not be Lewis's most admiring biographer but, in reacting to the film in a newspaper review, he cited item after item that was complete fiction. Lewis was not a glamorous movie star don – Sir Anthony Hopkins again – but an unattractive, chain-smoking, hard-drinking man with masochistic tendencies. Gresham was not an attractive and outgoing woman but a loud American devoid of social graces and with a taste for four-letter words in public. Lewis's real brother was not an engaging Dr Watson figure but a helpless alcoholic. There was no angelic small boy but two awkward teenagers in a house wracked with arguments and unhappiness. The love of Lewis and Gresham was, by most accounts, born of the mortification of the flesh, until she died of cancer and Lewis elevated her by his literary skill into the most sublime object of human affection. To this extent it was a love triumphing not just over cancer but over squalor, ugliness and domestic conflict.

In my view this would have made an even more moving and certainly more original film. It would also have been true to life. The film's apologists protest, with Keats, that 'beauty is truth, truth beauty' and that 'For ever wilt thou love and she be fair'. Even Mr Wilson, in cataloguing the historical errors in *Shadowlands*, finds himself concluding that perhaps they do not matter. 'Lewis existed very largely in the realms of fantasy . . . There is a strange sense in which the greater the falsehood the greater the truth.' I therefore run the risk of seeming prissy and pedantic.

Yet had Sir Richard Attenborough wished to attain Keats's state of grace, he had only to drop the claim to truthfulness, change the name of his characters and let beauty be its own path to truth. The story would have stood as fiction, and been the more 'true to life' as such. There is no shame in fiction. It has told us some of the greatest messages in all literature. But the concept of the 'documentary' has achieved a similar status to sex and violence. It is seductive and sellable. As such, film-makers claim a licence to play fast and loose with it. They lie to the public.

Another new film was *In the Name of the Father*. This was based on the unsound convictions of the Guildford Four in an IRA pub bombing case. Like *Shadowlands* it is a story well acted and well told. But it too professes to be telling the truth, of 'one of the most significant miscarriages of justice in the Western world this century'. That grandiloquent and questionable claim put me on my guard from the start. The turning point in the plot is a moment when the defence solicitor (played by Emma Thompson) manages to find her client an alibi for the night of the Guildford bombing. Hair aflame with anger, she screams at the Old Bailey judge, whose own words on film are taken from the official court report. Thompson's words are pure fiction, but are lent verisimilitude by being juxtaposed with those of the judge. The film nowhere indicates the truth, that the alibi she was quoting was not found by her but given to the defence by other police investigating the case. As for solicitors speaking in court at the Old Bailey, they do not. Advocates wear wigs not well-coiffed tresses. Nor did Conlon and his father share a cell in prison, nor were a dozen other central claims of the film true. It is, as the campaigner for the same cause, Robert Kee, pointed out, 'a farrago of rubbish'.

The defence of the director of *In the Name of the Father*, Jim Sheridan, was that his virtuous purpose justified his use of distortion and fiction. I suppose that was what the Guildford police said on the night of the arrests. Sheridan's film sets out to blacken British justice and damn the police. The story of the Guildford Four is a reasonable case history for that goal. But why, when their story has been so thoroughly researched and documented, not tell it as it was? There was no shortage of graphic horror. Sheridan told *Empire* magazine, 'We're absolutely unequivocally trying to influence the public . . . I can't draw conclusions, I can only put the facts as I know them.' But he does not put the facts. He puts lies. He makes up scenes and gives a star role to the Emma

Thompson character because she is a star actress. I imagine a younger Mr Sheridan would have castigated Hollywood for just such liberties with history. He has fallen into the same trap as the Guildford police, of deciding on his verdict and then seeking any means to substantiate it, however deceptive.

There have been excellent films about the troubles in Northern Ireland. One such was *The Crying Game*, which contrived to tell an important story without pretending to write history. Barry Diller's *Washington Behind Closed Doors* was, in my view, the best film on Watergate, better by far than supposed documentaries such as *All the President's Men*. Oliver Stone's *JFK* sought to prove that a second assassin was involved in the Kennedy murder and that the subsequent investigation led to a travesty of justice. Stone had the same difficulty that others have had in sustaining the conspiracy thesis. So he intercut true material from newsreels with scenes that he made up himself, for instance courtroom scenes involving his hero, Garrison. The result was a travesty of the truth. Stone and Sheridan both appear to have decided that the evidence of history was not enough for the cinema. It had to be polluted by fiction and bias. Neither was honest enough to warn the viewers of this intention. Both pretended to be telling history as it happened.

Facts are elusive things, as every journalist knows. Getting them wrong is quicker, simpler and usually makes a more lively story than getting them right. Fiction is free, facts are expensive. No wise newspaper promises to tell the truth, but I believe that most do at least mean to do so. The newspaper's motto is 'the first stab at truth in the time available'. The journalist is merely holding the fort until the historian arrives. That is the bond of trust, however tenuously maintained, between writer and public. Break it and journalism disintegrates.

These film-makers do not mean to tell the truth. They are aiming for 'a' truth, as they are when creating fiction. But their raw material is actual events, real people. They are using journalism's licence card but refusing to accept the discipline that goes with it. They seem to have lost the confidence to

142

put fiction to the service of propaganda, the confidence of Wadja in *Ashes and Diamonds* or of Costa-Gavras in *Z*. They undermine the validity of documentary technique as they undermine the rectitude of their message.

Third onto my screen was Stephen Spielberg's much-lauded *Schindler's List*. I did not like this film, which seems stereotyped in its characterization and ritualized in its horror. But it was undeniably powerful propaganda. Spielberg traces the fate of a group of Polish Jews saved by a Nazi businessman from death in the concentration camps. The film includes dates, places, personal names and black and white photography, all designed to enhance the documentary force of the story. At the end of the film, the actors are shown visiting Schindler's grave holding hands with the survivors of those they portrayed. This is filmed in colour and is devastatingly sentimental. The claim of authenticity could not be more total.

I happened to see this film after seeing the others mentioned above. I knew it was based on Thomas Keneally's well-researched book on Schindler and that testimony had been taken for the book from many of those directly involved. I was ready to accept the film both as history and as propaganda. But how far could I really believe in it? Was Spielberg a signed-up member of the same Hollywood 'history club' as Attenborough and Sheridan? Did he believe any means justified the end? As a result, I unavoidably wondered whether some of the more vivid scenes in the film really happened. Did the train with the women and children in fact go to Auschwitz, or did Spielberg merely want to get a concentration camp scene into his story? Did Schindler really make a speech on liberation day, and did a rabbi sing? I am told that the answer to all these questions is yes. Great efforts were made to ensure the authenticity of each scene, so as to forestall questions such as mine.

Yet my faith in the genre had been sorely tried by the other 'documentary' films that had not bothered to make such efforts. Perhaps history can look after itself with the passage of time. But what are known as 'faction' or 'docudrama' films

143

seek more than a place on the history shelf. Most seek influence. They are propaganda. They wish to elevate or condemn those whom they glorify or accuse. They want to turn minds to their way of thinking. They are powerful and are treated as such, both by those who make them and by those who watch them. Such films, and the licence claimed by those who make them, are dangerous. They use the same techniques they so often deplore in their victims, techniques of exaggeration and distortion. As such, they degrade the force of truthful documentaries such as *Schindler's List*. Filmmakers cannot claim exemption from the disciplines to which others claiming to describe modern history must adhere, including journalists. I would like films either to respect the integrity of the documentary, or deal in fiction, as have the great masters of this genre. The film can attain the art of the play and the novel. Directors of fiction, and the screen writers and actors they employ, can play their games of light and shade. They can let their imaginations dance free, exaggerate or diminish character, invent and manipulate plot. They can be false with impunity and through falsity tell their own sort of truth.

18

BETTING OUR HEDGES

HEDGES ARE a British speciality. I am told that France has more miles of hedge than Britain but I do not believe it. A French hedge is a scruffy stretch of *bocage*. They have hedges in Switzerland, in Denmark, even in Texas. But these are mostly mere strips of monospecies, laid by farmers to divide land or protect crops. A British hedge is the maverick of the countryside. It is a fragment of antique landscape, abused, torn, hacked, bent this way and that but never quite tamed. A hedge is nature's black economy. A field or a wood may be planted, sprayed, fertilized and harvested. A hedge is what farming leaves behind. Everything that is wild in the flora and fauna of Britain must find refuge in these narrow defiles. Here the huddled masses have taken up squatters' rights. Here birds, mammals, reptiles, trees, shrubs, sedges, orchids and weeds are crammed together, a microcosm of nature, all travelling steerage. British hedges are best.

Yet can they survive the flail? As February turns to March and March to April, the yeomen of Britain have one thought on their minds. Should they grub, flail, poison or lay? Most are flailing. Drive along a Dorset lane or a Yorkshire highway and you will see a machine styled after Boadicea's chariot, with a scythe flying wildly at its side. The cutting arm does not clip and push back into place. It wrenches, hacks and tears. Everything in its path is savaged. As it passes, it leaves snapped branches, broken flowers, smashed birds' nests, gaping wounds of nature scotched and bleeding.

The yeomen are not alone. In a letter to *The Times*, the Clerk of Patching Parish Council in Sussex has raised the same question. Flailing, he said, was the cheapest way to meet the council's obligation to keep highways and byways clear for passing traffic. Hand-cutting a hedge was out of the question. It was too expensive. If hedges were to survive, there was no alternative to the flail. To this a reader, Mrs Elizabeth Ringe, gave a stirring reply. How could anybody flail a British hedge, she cried. 'The awfulness of the shredded trunks and grotesque shapes left behind is particularly tragic now the sap is rising. How can wild roses, guelder roses, blackberries, hawthorn, hazel and many other species recover from these horrendous onslaughts?' The flail was inhumanity to nature. Better dead than bled, she might have added.

There is no aspect of natural history as ancient or complex as a hedge. Woods can be replanted. Fields can be resown. Streams can recover and hills return to peat and heather. But ever since Max Hooper, the Pythagoras of hedgemanship, enunciated Hooper's Rule in 1970, hedges have been seen as the quintessence of the British landscape. Hooper's Rule stated that the age of a well-established hedge can be deduced by multiplying the number of tree species per 30 yards by 100. The rule is implausible. But parish and other records confirm that a three-species hedge will be 300 years old, a five-species hedge 500 years old and so on. Suburban garden hedges do not count. Most are regularly weeded and are of just one species, privet, yew or beech. The ecologist Oliver Rackham subjected Hooper's Rule to scrutiny in his study of English landscape. He concluded that elm hedges were exceptions and that something odd happened in Somerset and other corners with a distinctive local ecology. But in general the rule held good. For a new tree family to take hold in a hedge and establish a stable relationship with the existing residents takes a century. Hooper had done for hedges what dendrochronology had done for wood.

There is no doubt which species is currently dominant. The hawthorn is undisputed monarch of the hedgerow. Despite the advent of the flail it is a tough survivor and greets spring with a burst of Mayflower. W. G. Hoskins wrote of the moment each year when hawthorn's 'miles of snowy hedges reach perfection, so dense and far-reaching that the entire atmosphere is saturated with its bitter-sweet smell'. Next to the hawthorn grows the hazel. This is an alien from the Continent, supposedly spread along the waysides of ancient Britain by Stone Age migrants, eating its nuts and defecating its seeds under hedges as they went. Like the urine-nurtured stinging nettle, the hazel is a memorial to mankind's simplest functions. With the hazel came the blackthorn, the lime, the oak, the elm and the beech. They in turn brought the whole panoply of nature.

The hedge is no friend to agriculture. It is the home of weeds, tares and hungry birds. It obstructs lines of sight and impedes the movement of machinery. Above all it occupies land. The history of farming is the history of warfare between the farmer and the hedge. Hedge-grubbing is as old as enclosure. A tiny hand-mowed field could never lend itself to mechanized farming unless incorporated with its neighbours. A farming writer of 1764 remarked that 'hedges are universally bad . . . There is no more sudden and obvious improvement than an hedge removed.' Hedges also sheltered human vagrants. The *Oxford English Dictionary* portrays them as the liberty halls of the open air: hence hedge-hopper, hedge-creeper, hedge-lawyer, hedge-poet, hedge-wedding, hedge-whore. The roadside hedge was habitat to the migrant hordes of pre-industrial Britain. There they rested, slept, loved and frequently died. Visitors to rural India today can see a similar sight. The hedge is the universal latrine.

To those of a romantic temperament, these features make the hedge all the more appealing. Few of Constable's landscapes omit a hedge. Keats saw the hedge as home to those ceaseless 'poets of the earth', the grasshoppers and crickets.

147

When summer birds were 'fainting silent' in the trees, 'a voice will run from hedge to hedge about the new-mown mead'. Hedges also were the nursery of trees. A grubbed hedge meant death to a hundred infants. John Clare wailed: 'Ye banish'd trees, ye made me deeply sigh/Inclosure came and all your glories fell.' Nor was the resulting landscape any better: 'The storm beats chilly on its naked breast/No shelter grows to shield, no home invites to rest.'

The post-war dominance of agricultural politics over other landscape concerns led to the grubbing-out programme subsidized by the Ministry of Agriculture in the 1960s and 1970s. It was the hedgerow equivalent of Mao Tse Tung's notorious 'war on the birds'. Hooper's Rule has since been invoked to show that the thousands of miles of hedges destroyed at the time were not Victorian plantings, as many farmers claimed, but went back to Saxon and even prehistoric times. The destruction was a conservation catastrophe. Its impact on flora and fauna was never assessed in advance. While nature is always resilient, the loss of species must have been huge. The BBC programme *Farming Week* used to open with a breakfast at which farmers would boast of how many miles of hedge they had torn up with government grants that year. I wondered if the BBC would allow developers a programme to boast their demolition of historic buildings.

It has been estimated (it can only be an estimate) that some 500,000 miles of hedges survived in Britain at the start of the grubbing-out campaign. By the time it was ended in 1983, between a third and a half had vanished. The geographer Richard Muir has calculated that in the county of Huntingdonshire alone, ten miles of Victorian hedgerow per square mile was down to three miles by 1965. A different survey by the Institute of Terrestrial Ecology, relying on aerial photography, suggests that the national total was down from half a million after the war to 360,000 miles in 1977, to 341,000 miles in 1984 and 267,000 miles in 1990. This is a staggering rate of loss. If archaeological sites were disappearing at this rate, and with taxpayers' money, there would be a national outcry. Yet hedges are the archaeology of nature.

The grubbing-out campaign has now stopped and there is even talk of grants being available for replanting. Such is the lunacy of government.

So what to do with the flail? *Times* correspondents were not unanimous. While many deplored the oozing stumps of broken shrubs, others saw flailing as the only way of keeping hedges in being. Mr Lowe of Kent wrote that 'the flail cutter is probably the main reason for the retention of the huge mileage of hedges we see left today'. Flailing was preferable to the only mechanical alternatives, spraying with poison or removal altogether. Hand-sawing was possible but too labour-intensive. But the Clerk of Patching was on Mrs Ringe's side. He had been able to use an 'innovation fund' to train 14 good men of Patching to 'cut and lay' 400 yards of old hedge a season. The skill, for which he had found ready takers, was known in those parts as brishing, probably a corruption of brushing.

One of the principal hedgerow custodians is British Rail. It has no doubt about flailing. Beset by commuters furious at 'leaf slips' caused by impacted leaves on its rails, BR wields more flails than any servant of the Crown since Wellington's flogging masters. Railway hedges were once kept in order by gangs of navvies or by the cinders falling from steam engines and burning back the undergrowth. Old photographs of steam engines passing through cuttings show slopes denuded of vegetation, usually by manual slashing and burning. Today BR has a dozen special rail-borne flailing trains and is proud of its target of 50,000 trees to be removed from 60 'vegetation blackspots' over the next decade. Its tree expert, Paul Knipe, says that flailing has taken over from spraying because, quite simply, it is more effective and is also kinder to the environment. 'Once a five-metre strip is established,' he says, 'the flail does not penetrate a hedge or disturb its internal ecology. The torn ends look ugly for a week or two but they lead to multiple regrowth, especially at this [spring] time of the year.'

These are murky waters. The implication of Mr Knipe's remarks is that flailing is actually the best form of hedge conservation. It is preferable to the chainsaw or the axe.

Despite its apparent crudity, it produces faster and thicker regrowth from the torn stump than traditional cutting and laying. It does not 'intervene' as drastically as manual hedging and over time produces a denser interior. This actually leads to greater protection for the wildlife within. The same is said of the deer, that it leaves the dense thorn alone but wrenches off sapling branches when they grow too long. They are natural coppicers. BR's way is thus nature's way.

I can hear the burghers of Patching protest that if you believe BR you will believe anything. On the other hand Mr Knipe makes sense. Nothing was more horrible than the corridor of dead and yellowed vegetation along a poisoned railway track. If it is poisoning versus the flail, I would opt for the flail. And while a hedge tended by hand may be a hedge loved and preserved, I have seen hedges 'cut and laid' so drastically as to be thoroughly traumatized. Flailing is a surface wound, a grander version of the privet owner's hedging sheers.

At least this is an argument among the converted. Hedges are once more cherished. I am told that they are even on the increase. A great calamity is being rectified. Both the flails of BR and the billhooks of Patching have their place in this campaign. It may take a hundred years, but sooner or later the hedges will return.

And on to Other Things

19

HOOKED, LINE AND SONATA

'NOW DON'T any of you tell me,' bellowed the disc jockey like a regimental sergeant major, 'don't you tell me you didn't ENJOY that!' That, I believe, was a fragment from Schubert's *Rosamunde*. 'That was great,' he continued. 'GREAT is the only word for that, or I'm not an Irishman.' He then discussed a horse that was a dead cert for the 2.30 at Cheltenham.

There is, I am told, a piece of string inside my radio which links the tuner knob to the dial. This year it was worn out. Day after day I have sent it spinning along the VHF waveband on a cacophonous journey from 90.2 FM to 100 FM and back. For me and four million others, 1993 was a year of indecision: to run off with the promiscuous young Classic-FM or to stay faithful to the old trouble and strife, BBC Radio Three.

My introduction to Classic-FM was love at first sound. I had long fantasized about my ideal music station. It would be 24-hours-a-day Schubert. I would awaken to impromptus and light piano pieces. The day would progress through the orchestral repertoire. Teatime would bring in the *Lieder*. Then the fare would become more refined, with chamber works and sonatas as the evening wore on. Familiarity would never breed contempt. As H. L. Mencken remarked, Schubert 'hatched more good ideas in 31 years than the rest of mankind has hatched since the beginning of time'. How Lord Clark could have omitted him from his pantheon of civilization I shall never know. This freest of spirits, this first great Impressionist, would have an ethereal beam entirely to himself. It would be a Turner Gallery of the air.

Classic-FM was not this to a T. It appeared to have borrowed from Rossini: 'Take Beethoven twice a week, Haydn four times a week and Mozart every day.' Its policy was simply to dump onto the transmitter just about every piece of classical music with even the remotest hint of familiarity to it. The playlist was 50,000-strong, selected by Robin Ray. This was then given an overlay of jazzy jingles, advertisements and ceaseless disc jockey banter. Beethoven's Fifth (fantastic!) would merge into Handel's *Water Music* (teriff!) and on into the *Trovatore* anvil chorus (wow!) and Mendelssohn's violin concerto (masterful!). Announcers would be all at sea. 'That was the great, er, Artu-rio Toscanini with Lascar Heifitz,' declared one. They were members, I guessed, of the feared 'Fingers' Paganini mob.

This was not just a down-market culture club. It was down-market with panache. Every piece was 'the world's most beautiful music', brought to air not by the muse of St Cecilia but by *Time* magazine, also the 'world's greatest'. On Saturday mornings there was a classical top-of-the-pops programme, a bizarre mixture of 'best bits' compilations and little-known composers from Poland and the film world. Stars listed their favourite works. Listeners wrote in with their most romantic moments. Evenings were given over to complete operas and orchestral concerts. It was immediately popular.

Immersing myself in all this was an extraordinary experience. I was relieved to have a station that treated its listeners not as prisoners trapped in a hall on uncomfortable seats but as they were, busy people with things to do, moving about their house or office, driving their cars, delighting to catch an old tune in passing. For me these were old acquaintances, long avoided for fear of over-indulgence. I had forgotten just how good was Strauss's *Emperor* waltz. I had not heard the mad scene from *Lucia* for years. It was a joy to rediscover

154

works I never hear nowadays in the concert hall, that are confined to dusty LPs in my attic: Beethoven's 'Leonore' No. 3, Handel's Largo, Chabrier's *España*, Chopin's better-known nocturnes. All had been lost in a Bermuda triangle, justly popular works from which I had averted my ear for fear of them becoming trite. Now I was suddenly bombarded with past loves. Here was my first study piece, 'the immensely talented Wolfgang Amadeus Mozart' and his 'little night music'. I realized I had not heard it since childhood.

Part of the shock was that Radio Three had for so long given no quarter in this direction. Its directors had rejected the top of the pops concept. They claimed that the world's most beautiful music was already in every listener's record library. They offered the next most beautiful music, even I suspected the least most beautiful music. From this it was a short step to the dame school programming of Radio Three's 'new brutalist' period, under William Glock and John Drummond. They firmly rejected Beecham's plea, that music should penetrate the ear with facility and quit the memory with difficulty. Glock produced the famous knuckle sandwich, of two lesser-known works by familiar composers wrapped round a first-broadcast performance by an unknown.

To me the BBC saw its audience as sitting by an ancient Bakelite wireless in slippers and cardigan, Horlicks in hand and cat in lap, waiting for the overture, concerto, symphony sequence as if they had nothing else to do. Presenters would intone in ecclesiastical voices the minutiae of a work's musical structure and the part of Vienna in which it was first performed. They were serious students of music and expected the audience to be the same. This was radio talking up to its listeners with a vengeance. When talk was required as a relaxation, the BBC would permit an arts administrator to come on the air to tell of his or her 'funding crisis'. The atmosphere of in-group was stifling.

I had no problem with the concept of a club. Radio Three inherited the mantle of the old Third Programme, a remarkable institution dedicated to high quality radio music, drama and talks. Its market was small but fiercely loyal. Then at some point in the 1970s it lost its way. The club became more introverted – I hate the abused word, élitist – and mostly deserted the spoken word. In presenting music it lost sight of what I can only call the quality of enthusiasm. I like classical music and enjoy listening to it for much of my day. Somehow Radio Three never made me want to listen through its ears.

In his *Music and the Mind*, Anthony Storr remarks that musical experts can become so close to their material that music as such ceases to be an object of love. Such people, he says, 'no longer play music or listen to it. For them music has become a scholastic endeavour devoid of emotional significance.' As Storr points out, a new piece of music is like a new acquaintance. It demands time and patience to get to know it. Most of us do not want new acquaintances pushed in front of us all the time. We want our encounter with music to be primarily a serendipitous meeting with old friends. Classic-FM seemed to understand this. It understood that broadcast music makes different demands on the listener from concert-hall music. This is surely why difficult or unfamiliar pieces are so much easier to grasp when the listener is sitting attentive in a hall in the presence of the players. All the senses must be committed to the task of appreciation, as Proust understood when he hired a string quartet to play to him alone.

For the same reason I find televised concerts so rarely satisfactory. On television the concentration of the ear is distracted by the concentration of the eye as the camera moves restlessly from conductor to background and from one player to another. I am not able, as in the concert hall, to rest my eye in one place or just gaze at the ceiling. I become engrossed in the musicians' appearance, their dress, the flowers in the room, the fingering on the instrument. Pictures always dominate sound. As anybody knows who appears on television, viewers remember what you wore and whether you smiled, seldom what you said. Sound radio requires the focus of a single sense, that of hearing. For this reason, Marshall McLuhan in *The Medium is the Message* described radio as

156

a hot medium and television as a cold one. Radio was potent because the listener had to be alert to attend to it. Television required only a descent into somnolent absorption. A dictator should use radio to gain power, said McLuhan, and television to keep it.

Broadcast music lets our bodies continue in action without losing mental application. It lets us do two things at once. Few listeners (except perhaps motorway drivers) have the occasion to give a radio station undivided attention. Broadcast music is not wholly distracting, as broadcast speech can be. It can accompany writing or reading. It is what Satie called *musique d'ameublement*, music in the background. Proust would have abhorred it.

Classic-FM took all this to heart. It wrenched radio music away from professional musicians and musicologists. It acknowledged that some pieces are more popular than others, and therefore merit more frequent playing. It brought to the marketing of the classics the techniques of popular music. This brought orchestral playing into thousands of homes that would never have appreciated it before. Sales of CDs rose and middle-brow composers achieved a new prominence, such as Michael Nyman, Górecki and those writing for television, the theatre and the church. Even the saccharine Classic Romance series recognized that, for many listeners, music is the medium that evokes and recalls their most intimate moments. What is wrong with that concept? Mozart would have cheered.

Yet I must temper my enthusiasm. As the months passed I admit to wearying of the fray. In the first place, Radio Three did not take the assault lying down. It hit back. Nicholas Kenyon, a lively music writer, had already been hired in 1992 to stave off the threat of a new classical station. He suggested to his staff that some of their listeners tuned in on the move and might therefore want something shorter and more accessible than the normal fare. To many at the BBC, this was heresy. Let the Sierra-driving Tchaikovsky-loving proles go out and buy cassettes, came the reply. The gossip was that Kenyon was 'not one of us'. The licence fee was not for enjoyment but for the elevation of the soul.

Kenyon fought back. After decades of monopoly of classical music broadcasting, Radio Three suddenly found it had just 3 million listeners to Classic-FM's 4.5 million. Something had to be done. Presenters became more chatty and personable. Movements from symphonies and arias from operas were no longer banned. The day began, as did the early evening, with 'highlights' programmes, including the excellent Brian Kay show. Unfamiliar and difficult works were kept more to the afternoon ghetto. Radio Three showed itself less afraid of the taste of its audience, less obsessed with advancing the work of a London musical coterie.

At the same time Classic-FM began to pall. Its jingle, despite being recorded in a dozen different modes by the Royal Philharmonic Orchestra, started driving me to distraction, or at least to the off button. The presenters seemed increasingly out of character with the music, inhabiting a world of Corfu holidays, Black Magic chocolates and 'name-a-Milan-opera-house' quizzes. Some may like their Bach partitas intercut with racing tips and quickie recipes, but not me. Fidelio's Radio Three prisoners had been let into the light and were indeed joyful. But after they had heard Vivaldi's *Spring*, Don Giovanni's champagne aria and Alfredo's *Un dì felice* over and over again, they began to crave the darkness. *Nessun dorma* indeed.

Worse than this, far worse, were the advertisements. Radio ads are true to McLuhan. They are hot. Heard once they sink in and that is enough. They cannot be ignored as can television advertisements, by turning away or clicking the sound off. They are insistent and penetrating. When repeated they are maddening. Those on Classic-FM were dreadful, apparently made by the junior staff in agencies whose star directors worked in television. Clients such as Multi-York furniture, Mercury phones, the NSPCC and the Barbados Tourist Office were presented in plummy accents by actors reading theatrical scripts that would have discredited a fourth former. On American classical music stations, dramatized advertisements are normally not permitted, nor can music be played adjacent to the station's own musical output. Adver-

158

tisements on Chicago's WFMT or Washington's WGMS are read by the presenters themselves in normal voices. Classic-FM staff acknowledged the poor quality of their advertisements and rather desperately held competitions for better ones. But they needed the advertisers' money and beggars could not be over-choosy.

The truth is that my musical taste is as yet unmet. I like the new Radio Three most of the time. I still flirt with Classic-FM between the ads. But up in the radiophonic ether, the free market has yet to answer my need. Music is 'all of Heaven we have below' said Addison, but its gods are not in my temple. One day, I hope, I shall punch in my requests at any hour of the day or night and some celestial beam will grant my wish. I shall at last have Radio Schubert. Until then, I must spin my dial back and forth into the night, restlessly seeking the sublime.

20

BOXING RINGS

I THOUGHT I was hallucinating. Emerging from Charing Cross Station on a bright spring morning I thought I saw a row of my beloved red phone boxes. They were planted right across the road towards St Martin-in-the-fields. They gleamed in the sun as if new and had the little crowns fashioned in their canopy picked out in gold. I turned and looked right down the Strand. There were more red telephone boxes. I looked left. A phalanx of boxes led my way into Trafalgar Square. In the square itself were yet more of these apparitions. They lined the wall of South Africa House. Suddenly I saw them everywhere I turned. Was this a film-maker's stunt, or a brilliant early birthday present to me, or had there been a *coup d'état* at British Telecom?

These kiosks were supposedly anathema. BT had hated them. The mere sight of one would give its modernist chairman, Sir Iain Vallance, the shudders. Red telephone boxes were to him what steam engines were to Dr Beeching. They symbolized that creature of greatest corporate loathing, the previous regime. BT had even rid itself of the name British Telecom and become just two initials in a frenzy of past-denial. As for the previous regime but one, the Post Office, ughh.

160

To BT the red phone boxes were archaic. Their image was of bakelite handsets, telephone operators in shawls and granny glasses, and 'Push button B'. They were set in concrete that stank of urine. Their huge doors were hard to open. 'Challenged groups' found them hard to use. Worst of all, they were old. The Vallance BT was to be a sunny landscape of digitized communication. It would have a logo. Prancing maintenance men kissing pan pipes would spread out across the nation bringing the good word that BT was new. They would touch each red box with a wand and in its place would spring up an easy-to-clean, plasticated black-and-yellow booth. Yellow was to be the 'international colour code of telecommunication'. The Vallance booths would be outer space calling modern person. They were the future.

We are now in that future and the booths are awful. Five years of familiarity with them has bred nothing but contempt. Even as telephone stands, they are noisy and leave the wind whipping about the feet. Apparently they were designed to have a life of no more than 15 years. The Scott kiosks had survived, with little serious maintenance, for over 50 years. The sheer glass of the new booths had become a gallery for call-girl stickers which nobody feels obliged to clean off. I met some Japanese tourists who assumed the booths were dedicated to this service. This was uncharacteristic British explicitness, they said. On every corner in the land was a prostitute contact centre, symbolized by a dancing male blowing his trumpet. But what, they asked, did BT stand for?

As art the booths are worse. There is no more miserable or more public monument to the exhaustion of British design patronage. The booths were acquired off the shelf from an American equipment supplier. Thus was a central component of the British streetscape torn out and replaced. Even Mercury's ogival canopies, equally garish in their pale blue colouring, have more style. Set on a housing estate or put down under a sodium light by a highway, the BT booths exaggerate bleakness. Set against a Georgian town wall, against any expanse of brick or stone, they are an architectural outrage. Not one minute of thought can have gone into their siting.

Sadly, 'small buildings' had been excluded from conservation area and other planning controls, an exclusion which BT exploited to the full. Across London, new booths were erected in Bloomsbury squares and facing Georgian terraces.

At the end of his television series on civilization, Kenneth Clark turned abruptly to the camera and launched into his final soliloquy. He asked himself what it was that defined a civilized community, that made it distinct from barbarism. His answer has always remained in my mind. The word, he said, was courtesy. The quality of courtesy was 'the ritual by which we avoid hurting other people's feelings by satisfying our own egos'. It was only through the conventions of human intercourse, of tolerance and good manners, he implied, that genius can flourish. Courtesy is essential to the good life.

I believe the same courtesy applies to those whose decisions order the pattern of cities – and whose egos so often disorder them. In Carey Street in London, at the back of the Strand Law Courts, stand four magnificent red kiosks as designed by Giles Gilbert Scott. Two are of the original K2 pattern, with which Scott won the Post Office competition for a new box in 1924. They are described by Alan Powers in his Thirties Society monograph on the kiosks as 'stately, temple-like and thoroughly architectural', with almost square window panes, fluted corners and a domed roof, inspired by the work of Sir John Soane.

The other two are examples of Scott's more common K6 'Jubilee' kiosks of 1935, slightly smaller refinements of the K2. They are set symmetrically in front of G. E. Street's exquisite iron screen, like twin fathers and twin sons. Behind them rises the polychrome Gothic façade of the Law Courts. The juxtaposition of ancient and relatively modern is inspirational. This is London design at its most elegant and robust. Round the front, in the Strand, similar boxes were ripped out and replaced with BT booths tucked uncomfortably under a colonnade. The result is a tawdriness utterly out of keeping with one of the city's grandest buildings. Only Lord Clark's barbarians could have put such objects in this place, only somebody steeped in the aesthetic discourtesy of a large organization.

Six years ago frantic efforts by English Heritage and a handful of local councils secured the listing for preservation of just over 2,000 red kiosks nationwide. Retention was agreed by BT grudgingly and only where the kiosks were 'sensitively sited' or in 'heritage locations'. I was intrigued at the implied converse, that the rest of Britain could be treated 'insensitively'. Since then a fury of destruction has consumed almost every red box in Britain. Of 60,000 Scott kiosks surviving in 1985, only 18,000 were still standing in 1993. Each day more were executed in the cause of corporate modernism.

Many boxes then experienced an extraordinary half-life. Gathered into depots, they were sold through scrap merchants. Some emerged as shower cabinets, drinks dispensers, phone boxes even. A correspondence in *The Times* revealed sightings of boxes in Malta, Zimbabwe, Hong Kong and Los Angeles. There were boxes outside the *Queen Mary* in San Diego and by London Bridge in Arizona. They were collector's items. They passed the test of true design, they had a value in themselves. They still feature prominently in tourist picture postcards.

So what is happening in Westminster? The answer is that the city council has told BT that it does not like the new booths. If BT wants to install any new telephone boxes in the city's conservation areas they must be Scott ones. In particular it wants Scott ones only on what is termed the 'ceremonial route' from the Law Courts in the Strand down to Trafalgar Square and along Whitehall to Westminster. Hence my apparition. Why this particular route should be so blessed is unclear. The route is rarely used for ceremonial purposes and when so used, it is unlikely that monarchs, mayors or legislators would suddenly stop their carriages to make a call from a K6. I must assume that visiting dignitaries are likely to be so offended by the new booths that their senses must be protected from them. The crowns set into the canopies have been painted gold in their honour. Sixty-two such boxes are to be installed in all. There appear to be two every 20 yards. Like policemen in dangerous parts of town, they stay in pairs for security.

Thank goodness for such mercies. The early Scott kiosks, with Soanian arches for roofs and neo-Georgian glazing bars, were intended not just as cubicles for commerce. They were designed as part of the London scene by one of the most distinguished architects of the time, creator of Battersea power station and Liverpool Cathedral. Their concession to corporate identity was both simple and sufficient. They were red. That red, 'pillar box red', became London red, adorning the glorious triumvirate of post box, double-decker bus and telephone kiosk. The grey-black interwar city was brought to life by these daring innovations. They were instantly popular because they were beautiful and settled easily in the mostly-classical London streets. No painting or photograph of London was or is complete without a splash of this red.

One indicator of the collapse of metropolitan confidence is the collapse of control of public design. London buses today are no longer all red, and some are defaced by ugly advertisements. Taxis no longer need be black or other restrained dark colour. They too can be covered in advertisements, including hideous whites, yellows and pinks. These breach a former regulation prohibiting trade vehicles carrying advertising from using roads in the royal parks. Like graffiti, these changes imply a loss of authority, an intimation of anarchy. They suggest nobody cares.

I find myself ambivalent about this. Government interferes too much in too many private activities. Yet the design of cities is the most public of all domains. The look of a city street, like the conservation of old neighbourhoods, can only be ordered by the community through some collective discipline. That is what time and again the community indicates that it wants. The trouble in London is that central government has assumed local government functions in big matters, such as roads and public transport. But it regards ostensibly trivial London-wide functions such as restrictions on building height, on the appearance of the Thames or on taxis, buses and phone boxes, as beneath its dignity.

There was no reason why a new kiosk should not have been designed, for new sites or even to sit alongside the old boxes as the K6 sits alongside the K2s by the Law Courts. Urban design must admit the new. Scott's kiosk was once new, having won the commission in an open competition. The BT booth won no competition and was, I understand, not even the subject of design discussion with BT. It boasts no author. It could not even be called ugly, since ugliness can often be the starting point to beauty. The booth is too bland to be ugly. It derives its ugliness from its relations with its setting. Ugliness is imposed by it on its surroundings. That is what can and must be retrieved. Bernard Shaw called for public art to be motivated by 'the might of design, the mystery of colour, the redemption of all things by Beauty'. This challenge was met by Giles Gilbert Scott and in the matter of telephone kiosks has not been bettered. The BT booth is no match.

In a well-governed community these mistakes would be avoided. Design consciousness would become design conscience. BT has no such conscience and there is no government entity to exercise it on London's behalf. The result, in Westminster, is that planning discipline must eventually be exerted, with help from public opinion, after the event and at a cost. At least it is being exerted. The new booths are supposed to last only 15 years. The red telephone box is fighting back. It is not dead and may be on the brink of revival. It is no hallucination.

21

THE LOUVRE MANOEUVRE

WHICH IS the world's greatest art gallery? The old party game has lost none of its vitality. The Metropolitan pits its Vermeers against Washington's Goyas. Amsterdam throws its Rembrandts at Vienna's Breughels. The Pitti shows Botticelli to Madrid's Velasquez. London has its glorious cocktail in Trafalgar Square. But over them all looms Paris. Every time that emporium of art on the banks of the Seine seems to lose a battle – recently to London's Sainsbury wing – it returns with a thunderous barrage.

Museums are the pilgrimage churches of our age. Visitors travel vast distances to worship at these shrines, bound together by a common canon. In buildings throughout Europe and North America are roughly comparable collections of paintings from the Renaissance to the Impressionists. Entering these vaults the pilgrim is at once at home. The ritual is familiar, the emblems are recognizable, the liturgy can be recited by heart. Like the great churches, these museums are rich. Concentrated within their walls is more wealth than anywhere else on the face of the earth. This has its own magic, and its own architecture of extravagance.

Within four weeks of the opening of the Louvre's Richelieu wing on the Rue de Rivoli at Christmas 1993, almost a million people visited it, and reeled away stunned. The guidebook admonished them. Six months are apparently required for full obeisance at the feet of the goddess Louvre. The true acolyte will do his penance at leisure. The new wing alone has the floor area of the British Museum. The route to Santiago de Compostela is an afternoon stroll in comparison. Why is it that the French can build such monuments and the British cannot?

Britain in the past ten years has added its modest grains of sand to the edifice of art exhibition, for instance the Sainsbury wing of the National Gallery, the Clore wing of the Tate and the Courtauld Gallery at Somerset House. These are handsome displays. But they are nothing alongside Paris's stupendous work. The difference lies in political leadership. The Grand Louvre, as the whole Louvre restoration project is called, was personally ordered and supervised in 1981 by the French president, François Mitterrand. He brooked no opposition and quibbled at no expense. The Louvre was just one of many *grands projets*. Others were a new national library, a new opera house at the Bastille and a science park. The Musée d'Orsay across the Seine was similarly commanded by the president's predecessor, Giscard d'Estaing. In Britain only Dockland railways and Malaysian dams benefit from such prime ministerial droit de seigneur over the Treasury.

The Richelieu wing is an architectural sensation. I do not like I. M. Pei's pyramid in the Louvre central square. It is a crude intrusion and is becoming ever more scruffy. The space beneath it is a lobby to Hades, a bleak airport concourse without intimacy or relief. There is no picture, no poster, no statuary, nothing to relieve the exhaustion of visitors. They must wait in interminable queues to gain admission. This is big art crushing the human spirit, not uplifting it. Pei is also responsible for the Richelieu wing, but his architectural contribution is limited. He supplies a characteristically frigid basement area, complete with a gimmicky inverted pyramid, and has varied the ground floors of the two courtyards with inclined planes and slit windows. Why he has done this is a mystery. Modern museum architecture can supply visual richness and stimulus if the client wants it, as Robert Venturi did at the Sainsbury wing in London. Pei is an unreformed minimalist.

Pei at least does not seek to compete with the old building that rises above his basement and courtyards. Here are the façades and salons of Napoleon III's Louvre extensions, four storeys of splendour including a suite built for the French foreign ministry for the reception of distinguished guests and until recently occupied by the Ministry of Finance. They are restored and opened as a display of French 'Victorian' design and must be among the most magnificent nineteenth-century rooms in the world. On these upper floors also are the Louvre's Assyrian, Egyptian, Islamic and Gothic collections. Elsewhere are exhibitions of tapestry, jewellery and silverware from all periods. On the top floor is the crown of glory: new picture galleries for the museum's previously neglected Dutch, German and Flemish masters, as well as more space for French works. This is, in effect, a complete new National Gallery, comprising no fewer than 165 rooms.

I may have seen some of these paintings before but I had certainly not noticed them. One room after another is devoted to artists in which the Louvre was not thought to be strong, to Memling and Cranach, Ruisdael, Cuyp and Steen, Van Dyck and Rubens. There is Rubens *ad nauseam*. There are rooms filled with Poussins and Claudes. There is the picture I most covet of all, Holbein's *Erasmus at his Desk*. (If ever that picture is stolen, the art squad should search my study at once.) Directions and mapping are faultless. Pictures are well-described and set on softly-coloured backgrounds. Compared to the chaotic Musée d'Orsay, the Richelieu wing is order enriched by ostentation.

For whom have the French spent a sum believed to be approaching £750 million? The answer is clear. They have spent it for the enjoyment of the world and the glory of France in equal measure. They will get it back with interest. There is in Britain little point in pleading for cultural investment. What economists call the 'social rate of return' is too imprecise for government or commercial banker. The value is too unquantifiable. London's three new galleries were paid for entirely by private donors – Courtauld, Clore and Sainsbury. Government was not interested. Such expenditure was not its business.

The view taken by the French authorities could not be more different. Since the opening of the new Louvre five years ago, attendances have risen from three million to five million a year. Although ticket sales – no nonsense about free admission – cover just a fifth of total costs, constant investment in Paris's museums is regarded as crucial in keeping the city a premier tourist destination. Tourism is now Europe's most important international export. France is leading the charge and its government is out in front.

The proof of success is in the pudding. France's foreign tourism earnings rose in the course of the 1980s by 9 per cent, allowing for inflation. Britain's rose by 5.7 per cent, which implied a steeply declining market share. Britain's balance of payments on tourist account collapsed over the same decade, from a surplus of £688 million in 1979 to a deficit of £3.5 billion in 1993. At the same time, France's rose from £2 billion to £5 billion. I am sceptical of many statistics and always put on dark glasses and a crash helmet when consulting them. But these seem so devastating as to be notable. France is drawing the world's art pilgrims to its shores and there are millions of them. Britain is not.

Modern tourism depends on more than good hotels, railways and coach parks. True, most in-depth surveys conclude that Americans coming to Britain are set on three goals: shopping, shopping and shopping. But they also require there to be an initial magnet, a superficial reason for coming in the first place. In Britain's case this will never be the sun or beaches or water sports or skiing. Traditionally it has been the well-known round of historic buildings and towns – the Tower of London, Buckingham Palace, Stratford and York – and in London the musical stage, museums and art galleries. But few of these attractions bring second visits. Many

American cities have admirable galleries. Britain's country houses and historic towns are short of novelty value. Musicals now travel abroad. Another Lloyd Webber will not compete with another wing on the Louvre.

British arts projects seem locked in a rigor mortis. After years of government mind-changing, the British Library is now to be only half built. The National Gallery extension was a 40-year saga as long as the government wanted to build it itself. The Royal Opera House is trapped in one planning delay after another. The location of a London museum of modern art to replace the inadequate Tate is still an embarrassingly open question. A Frenchman would put it on Bankside, pay for it and have done with it.

This approach is not wholly without its virtues. The British are suspicious of grand gestures. Some of President Mitterrand's, such as the Bastille opera and the new library, are the butt of ridicule as ill-conceived and absurdly expensive. Britain has more affection for the small platoons, the parish churches, the country houses, the old villages and the theatres upstairs. We admire privacy and discretion and take pride in understatement. We can cheer when asked, as on Jubilees and D-Days. But we cheer *sotto voce*.

Yet even understatement needs its backer. Tourist investment in Britain is undertaken by operators at the coalface, by hotels, coaches, souvenir shops. They invest in their own businesses. They do not cross-subsidize the magnets that marked down Britain as a destination in the first place. These magnets – the tended countryside, historic houses and towns, theatres and museums – must grasp at such money as they can make from admission charges or grants for running costs. English Heritage has for ten years been unable to secure either the money or the planning consents to replace the grim visitor centre at Stonehenge. It is a public monument of great tourist appeal, for whose improvement the government disclaims all responsibility.

The French government acknowledges such responsibility in full and manages to fuse it with national pride. This fusion applies to every large investment, from a museum to a high-speed train to a well-maintained motorway. Ask a Frenchman if he feels the £750 million cost of the Grand Louvre money well spent (as he has been asked) and he will reply in the affirmative. That yes will partly reflect a love of art, but equally a love of country and a pride in French achievement. This love is unquantifiable and 'unfundable' but no less real for that. Governments must take a deep breath and pay up, even if this means paying ransom to the contractors and artists concerned – as at the Bastille opera.

British governments shy away from such expensive chauvinism. Enthusiasm is suspect in a minister, especially if it costs money. In Britain, political leadership is scrupulous not to sponsor public projects. The Treasury, the central institution of British government, pursues nothing with conviction except the next year's planned expenditure total. Its chief secretary might take his title from the Louvre's first custodian, the Chevalier de Non (who gives his name to one of the museum's three new wings).

Britain may match France in its appreciation of art and even its sponsorship of small galleries and museums. What the British lack is a political culture to transform this appreciation into the grand gesture. We scale down our ambition to concentrate on the little and the informal. We boast parish churches, rolling landscape, historic villages. We treasure stately homes and their collections, provincial galleries and 'working' museums. These lesser glories have their virtues. They may not make a big bang and are certainly harder to sell. They do not shout from the marketing brochure. But at least we know that we and our visitors can handle them. Britain's cultural attractions do not leave their audience bemused and exhausted, like competitors in some Japanese game show. They do not require huge investments for their display. Their pleasures are perhaps the more intense for being piecemeal.

What I cannot accept is defeat. I wish we could do one big thing well. Britain needs something new, a Sydney Opera House, an Empire State Building, an Acropolis, one

171

thumping great attraction of which the whole world will say, 'I must go and see that before I die.' Like Cyrano we should show that we can do something 'with panache'.

22

STOPPER AND PINTARD

Stoppard and Pinter, Pinter and Stoppard. Like Marks and Spencer or Morecambe and Wise, the British like to take their heroes in pairs. But we need to get the sequence in the right order. Sullivan and Gilbert would never have found fame and fortune. The couplings must scan. But couplings there must be, and this pair are the defining dramatists of our age.

Until recently I had my doubts. Both these great talents of the 1970s seemed to have been wrung dry by the experience of the 1980s. Others had come up on the rails. Bennett, Hare, Frayn and Ayckbourn, all produced plays that I believe will pass the test of time. S and P stuttered and fell silent, or occasionally produced work that was message without respect for medium, politics without presentation. Neither had a full-blown success in ten years. Both were dogged by that awful fear of the artist down the ages: 'They seem to prefer my early stuff.' The London audience is merciless. It points to the empty stage and frowns.

Suddenly in 1993 both were back, firing two barrels each in quick succession. A new play by Harold Pinter called *Moonlight* transferred to the Comedy Theatre in the West End after a sold-out run at the Almeida in Islington, where it

173

amassed a shelf of awards. At the same time Tom Stoppard's *Arcadia* filled the Lyttleton Theatre at the Royal National, also transferring to the West End. Meanwhile a series of Pinter revivals was capped by a brilliant production of *No Man's Land* (1975) with Paul Eddington and Pinter himself in the leading roles. Not to be outdone, Stoppard and Adrian Noble staged his heavily revised 1974 play *Travesties* at the Barbican. It too filled the house. Each writer can step forward and take a bow. They can cry: 'Not dead, My Lords, but merely sleeping ere the crowing of the cock.'

Both Pinter and Stoppard are famously sensitive souls. I am sure they hate being bracketed together, even in praise. They must be no less infuriated by glib comparisons often – and enjoyably – made between them. Pinter is the spare, difficult modernist; Stoppard the post-modern artist of theatrical rococo. Pinter is a minimalist, deep, hard, obscene, the embodiment of rage. Stoppard is rich to verbosity, classical, eclectic, subtle. Pinter's humour is black, with a sneer, Stoppard's is a drawing-room titter. While Pinter is pounding his fists on the bare boards of the fringe, Stoppard is luxuriating with the cherubs of the subsidized stage. They are contrasted as poets of heart and head, as tramp and dandy, rocker and mod.

Both writers attempted political drama in the 1980s. Pinter's decade culminated in the grim (to me unwatchable) *Mountain Language*, Stoppard's in a series of enjoyable but inconsequential tributes to friends, *Every Good Boy Deserves a Favour* picking up where *New-Found-Land* left off. Both had to endure the torture of constant interviews about writer's block. Now they have both managed to break free from the strait-jacket of the Thatcher era, a period that seemed to require of them a leaden political commitment. They are back in their *métier*, pushing, teasing, begging the English language into telling a story. The new plays are uncannily similar in style and content to the revived ones of the 1970s. It is hard to believe that two decades separate the two pairs of works.

I cannot deny that much of Pinter's *Moonlight* leaves me mystified. The plot is literally unexplained, not least the opening ghost sequence. I was never intrigued and soon ceased to care what happened to most of the characters. Yet at the play's heart lies a conversation between a dying man and his wife portrayed with intense poignancy by Ian Holm and Anna Massey. I could forgive the rest. This was what Pinter always did best, the lines without words, the reaching out for love yet not finding another to touch, the Corbusian architecture of human bleakness. There are even unexpected flashes of a more hopeful Pinter: 'I don't believe it's going to be pitch black forever,' says the dying Andy, 'because if it's pitch black for ever what would have been the point in going through all these enervating charades?'

Pinter takes Beckett and Kafka as his lodestars. I find him colder even than them, closer to the Scandinavians, to Strindberg and Ibsen. He is a theatrical Edvard Munch. But the pit into which he makes his actors look is not completely empty. The repetition of meaningless proper names may now have become a cliché, and the sudden shifts of accent and plot almost suggest a Pinter parodist. But the ability to sear the mind is undiminished. After *The Homecoming* in 1969, Pinter said that he 'couldn't any longer stay in the room with this bunch of people who just opened doors and came in and went out'. In *Moonlight* he returns to that same room and that same bunch of people. He is addicted to their company. He is clearly at home with them.

Stoppard has come home too. The 1980s had left him, as the critic John Russell Taylor put it, with that awful quality 'a sense of responsibility: Tin Man welds heart to sleeve.' Taylor admitted to preferring 'the rake unreformed, the joker unsobered'. *Arcadia* is a return to the same intellectual maze as preoccupied Stoppard and his audience in *Jumpers* and *Travesties*. The same surface learning, always verging on mere cleverness, is on display. In the opening scenes, Sheridan's *Rivals* has supplanted Wilde's *Importance of Being Earnest* as the dramatic metaphor and humour bank. Chaos theory has supplanted Dadaist art theory. An English country house with a couple of historians has supplanted a Zurich house occupied by a reminiscing diplomat. Byron and Capability

Brown have replaced Joyce and Lenin. But the dramatic choreography, the labyrinthine plot, the relentless quips, puns and quotations still have audiences digging each other in the ribs.

This is the old Stoppard talking up to his market. Did Byron flee England in 1809 after murdering a jealous husband? Did the daughter of the house accidentally invent the Second Law of Thermodynamics? Did her tutor become the hermit required by the picturesque architect? Will the prim archivist or the odious Sussex lecturer be the one that discovers the truth? Can the audience follow the jokes, let alone the plot? Stoppard is a branch of fractal geometry, a one-man journey into the far reaches of the Mandelbrot set. Will he return before the play ends?

At one level all Stoppard's work is high-class cabaret. The staging never allows the eye to wander. Actors suddenly break into dance. They adopt poses and change character so that we are never quite sure whether they or the director or Stoppard himself has quite made up their minds how to run a scene. In the 1993 *Travesties*, quite different from the 1974 original, we are left wondering whether Anthony Sher's revision of the John Wood part of Carr is by Sher or by Adrian Noble or by Stoppard. Just as the characters on stage are meant to mirror each other – when they are not travestying each other – so those involved in staging the play appear to be engaged in the same clever exercise. We are with Wilde all along: 'In matters of grave importance, style, not sincerity, is the vital thing.'

Likewise the audience's mind must be constantly on the alert. There is no quarter given to a lapse in concentration. Miss a clever allusion and we are wandering up a cul-de-sac while the play races elsewhere. This can impede enjoyment, as can the apparently indulgent plays on words. 'You'll be missing Sofia?' Carr asks the Rumanian artist, as Dadaism intertwines with Wilde. 'You mean Gwendolyn,' comes the reply. Drunk? 'Post hock, propter hock.' And on it goes. Stoppard has us smiling at each epigram. Yet before we can ponder its truth or daftness he is on to the next one.

Arcadia is the authentic post-modernist play. It is a comedy of manners and ideas and devoid of apparent message. Stoppard's old weakness is still there, his inability to handle romantic love. His linguistic electricity plummets to earth whenever his heroes cease their crackling repartee. The two Arcadian academics, Hannah and Bernard, sink into banality the moment their lines require them to direct their emotions towards each other. But this never lasts long and the intellectual optimism soon returns: 'It's the best possible time to be alive, when almost everything you thought you knew is wrong.' Stoppard bubbles on: 'For every thousand people, there's nine hundred doing the work, ninety doing well, nine doing good and one lucky bastard who's the artist.'

I prefer to see these two writers as a continuum rather than a contrast. At a certain stage along the theatrical road the coach comes to a halt. Stoppard leaves the driving seat and Pinter climbs into it. The good times are finished and the hard times begin. After a glorious sunset comes the dark. When Stoppard's party is over, when the jokes have had their chuckles, when every jumper has been travestied and every Hapgood deserved his favour, Stoppard is nagged by questions he cannot answer. 'When we have found all the mysteries and lost all the meaning,' says Septimus at the end of *Arcadia*, 'we will be alone, on an empty shore.' The universe is cooling, time is an arrow, only chaos obeys laws.

Stoppard's reaction is to brush aside the question. He invites Septimus and the audience to a luscious final waltz, an extraordinary gesture of stagecraft. But that is it. Had Hannah and Bernard ever decided, disastrously, to set up home together, Stoppard would have been at a loss. How would they have ended their days? They would have sent in despair for Dr Pinter. They would have grown into Andy and Bel, the anti-heroes of *Moonlight*, bleakly reflecting on their past, communicating with the audience but not with each other or with their children.

Pinter leads us away from Stoppard's waltz. He takes us into a freezing room, sits us down and tells us to ponder awhile in silence. 'What is being said here? . . . What finally

177

is being said?' asks Jake. By some theatrical trick, Pinter makes me look for answers to his merciless questions. Martin Esslin, in a study of his work, records the frequent criticism that Pinter 'lacks the wide sweep, the variety of subject matter and character which marks a major playwright, a Brecht, Shaw, Ibsen or Shakespeare; Pinter is no more than a miniaturist, a minor master with a narrow range.' Yet as Esslin points out, depth of insight as well as width of subject matter is equally the mark of greatness in a playwright. Authors whose main preoccupation is 'the inner life of man, his basic existential problems, which of necessity are few, have undoubtedly been of comparable stature.'

Hence Pinter's fascination with words, with the technicalities of human communication. Hence too his obsession with their inadequacy, reflected in silences, in abuse and in obscenity – his 'lines without words'. His texts are scattered with rows of three dots. He is meticulous that actors and directors respect them to the dot. This rigidity does not always help the actors or the audience. Pinter is on stage and nobody else. The drama reflects Pinter's anguish, his bleakness, his solemn wit. Despite the brilliance of his actors, I am never quite sure how far they 'add value' to the text. I do not like many of Pinter's plays. There are few that, once seen, I want to see again – certainly not *Moonlight*. Yet for all this qualification, I am moved by the experience.

One reason is that I admire Pinter's and Stoppard's passion for the English language. 'I don't think writers are sacred, but words are,' says a character in Stoppard's *The Real Thing*. Both are master craftsmen in English. Stoppard once compared an English sentence to the splicing of a cricket bat. Cricket is also Pinter's favourite pastime. They are sophisticated writers, although Stoppard was the child of Czech parents and Pinter's background was East London working class. Both seem to bring to the English sentence an outsider's sensitivity. They show a wonder at its magic that is rare in a native speaker. Neither went to university. Both learned to write 'on the job', Stoppard in Bristol journalism, Pinter on stage as an actor. Both careers require efficiency of language.

Future critics may see this pair as mere chroniclers of a morally anaesthetic age. (For a different comment they might turn to Alan Bennett.) Pinter and Stoppard may be dismissed as verbal technicians, manipulators of language, funny, clever but inconsequential. The difference between them may be seen as one of temperament. Both authors exploit the same magic: the game of verbal communication, the confusion of words with ideas, of ideas with people. Certainly they ask questions without necessarily giving answers. But the pleasure of the theatre is to ask such questions without clobbering the audience with answers, treating it with respect; allowing it to take over when the playwright departs.

Many critics of these two new plays have complained that both *Arcadia* and *Moonlight* look back not forward. When Stoppard and Pinter attempted to move ahead and wrestle with the politics of the Eighties, they fell on their faces. They have been forced to return to the old prison of the English lyric tradition of Sheridan, Wilde and Coward. To me this is their strength. I love the English lyric tradition. It is the glory of a language that dominates the globe. It has the most words, the widest range and the greatest flexibility. Its imagery offers the writer the richest of lexicons and a whole world ready to listen. Pinter and Stoppard are the first writers of English as a global tongue.

Here are two artists who have rediscovered their confidence, their talent to entertain and stimulate. The prodigals have returned to their proper home, the stage. All we demand is that they write more plays.

23

THE MARCH OF THE OLD CONTEMPTIBLES

WE GROW old. We remember too much and avoid the shock of the new. We yearn for a good drawing, a healthy likeness. We scorn the Hayward and the Tate. But some of us do keep trying. We keep banging our heads against the wall of what London's gallery directors offer us as modern art and we feel the lumps and the blood.

I went recently to the Hayward Gallery and gazed at what was presented as the cream of European sculpture between 1965 and 1975. The show was an assembly of neon tubes, light bulbs, sacks, old newspapers, a parrot, cactus, brushwood and piles of foam rubber. The catalogue said this expressed 'totality and matter of factness in relation to the viewer . . . The playfulness asks fundamental questions that are philosophical as well as physical.' I wondered what other corner of the public sector could get away with putting such gibberish into cold print at the taxpayers' expense. I simply could not make out what was going on.

The criterion by which somebody had chosen these objects, none of which had been worked or crafted, was a mystery. The exhibits could not be said to be good or bad 'art'. None of them had been made by what was recognizably an artist. They had simply been found and assembled. The quality of such displays can only lie in the mind of the selector, the curator of the gallery. He or she must deserve as much credit for the serendipitous collection as the so-called sculptor. Both are performing an identical act, that of picking up ordinary things and putting them on public show. The curator needs no sculptor as mediator, nor do the objects need a title. They could as well have been picked up from the street. To call such an enterprise artistic is meaningless.

I sought an antidote. At the Royal Academy was an exhibition of The Great Age of British Watercolours. I went three times, and each time it was more packed than before. The show was the blockbuster of the year, with some 2,500 visitors a day crammed into just six galleries. By comparison, New York's Matisse exhibition had handled twice that number over 30 galleries. The reason for the popularity was plain. The Academy had summoned from their lairs the Old Contemptibles of British art. The watercolour lobby had waited long for this day and meant to make the most of it. The art establishment would see what the foot soldiers could do when allowed a parade.

They came in their corduroys and tweeds, in their tartans and twills and sensible shoes. They jammed the cafeteria and put away acres of quiche. Students clutched their clipboards. Old ladies struggled with the huge catalogues. These people had learned about painting not in the frigid sheds of the art colleges. They had sat in the salons of the Courtauld, the attics of the National Trust, the basements of Abbott and Holder. They had fought off the sneers of abstract expressionists, minimalists and conceptualists. They had bunkered down under a hail of bricks, scrap metal, pebbles and junk. They had bided their time and stayed true to the faith. Now they were rewarded with the greatest names in the watercolour pantheon, Cozens and Girtin, Cotman and the Varleys, Cox, Turner and Palmer. I have rarely seen faces glow with such joy in an art gallery. Not here the bored yawns, the fingering of catalogues, the frowning search for the artist's name on the card. These people knew. As they floated from room to room theirs was the smile of recognition. They were among friends.

High priest of all this was Andrew Wilton, organizer of the exhibition. He had admittedly been cavalier. He seemed to have tossed onto the walls whatever pictures came easily to hand from the period 1750 to 1880. There was little by way of theme and scant regard for balance. The same artists cropped up again and again with little rhyme or reason. The show was a mess. But who cared? From the monochrome experiments of Cozens, Gilpin and Girtin to the sumptuous gouaches of Samuel Palmer and Turner's great exhibition pieces there was not a dull moment. This was the most glorious age of British art, in perhaps its most glorious medium. Even Gainsborough, Turner and Constable seemed more intense, more revolutionary, in watercolour. The medium offers a harsh discipline, instant in punishing error. For most of these artists, oil paintings were safe products, easy to market. Watercolour appealed to a private corner in their imagination. It was the medium for taking risks, or at least taking pains, as in Ruskin's meticulous shaping of a woodland leaf. Constable showed this in his cloud studies and Turner in his Italian washes.

The exhibition dripped with moisture. On one occasion I arrived in a downpour and had the sensation of looking at the pictures as if they were soaking wet. Perhaps water has always been the climatic veil through which the British see their landscape. Water seeped, dripped, ran, cascaded down the walls of the Academy. Turner's great picture of the Reichenbach Falls had me reaching for an umbrella. The washes of Cox and Bonington look as if they had been dipped in a stream and left to dry. Whistler's seascapes appear drenched with tears, as perhaps they were. When Danby or de Wint struggled to bring sunlight onto a wall or hillside, the foreground steams in protest and rainbows burst from heavy clouds.

Turner towered over the show. His view of Stamford High Street is one of his finest works in any medium. The studies of the Venetian lagoon, in which sun, air and water are stirred into pools of colour, are as good as anything he did in oil. But the revelation for me was John Sell Cotman. He emerged from the shadows of his black castles and lowering slopes to challenge the masters. He took up the mantle of the young Girtin and could have passed it straight to the Impressionists had he not wandered off into etching. His studies of Croyland Abbey, Greta Bridge and Chirk Aqueduct presaged Cézanne as Turner presaged Monet. Like Girtin, he found inspiration in the blacks and blues of the English landscape, in the thrill of a castle battlement or a church tower picked out by a ray of sun. He loved the dark. His painting of St Mary Redcliffe is not so much of the dawn rising as of the night all too reluctantly taking its leave. This is the art of the age of Wordsworth and Coleridge, and every bit as daring.

In among these heavyweights were the lesser contestants. Topographers such as Shotter Boys, Bonington, the Sandbys and Samuel Prout seemed to blossom in the reflected glory of the greats. Those recorders of exotic empire, Daniell and Roberts, were well represented. So too were the sunsets of John Martin, to which Queen Victoria was so attached. Samuel Palmer gave us his idylls of the Surrey and Kent gloaming. His *Harvesters by Firelight* came from the Mellon in Washington.

Finally in a room of their own were the works intended by these same watercolourists for public exhibition. Large paintings in gilt frames show them struggling to outdo oil painters in grandness of subject matter – mountain scenery, stags at bay, soldiers departing for war – and in vehemence of colours. These pictures lack the radicalism of the rest of the show. Watercolour was entering a competition it was unlikely to win, that of sheer size. The medium was no longer punching its weight. An episode was over. But what an episode.

Thus reinvigorated I found myself returning to the fray. I read an article in the *Financial Times* imploring readers to go and see what was described as 'one of the only pieces of successful monumental sculpture in London'. It was an entry for the annual Turner art prize, a prize claiming cultural

descent from the master himself. The prize was for painting
or sculpture. The piece in question was a sculpture, located
at the junction of Grove Road and Roman Road in E8. It
was on a shortlist which, in the view of the chairman of the
judges Nicholas Serota, offered 'new insights into the society
and culture in which we live and share'. Why, I wondered,
did art need to talk so big: was it nervous about something?

The sculpture was by a woman called Rachel Whiteread.
She had secured a stay of execution on a Victorian terraced
house that was being demolished to create an open space
next to a council estate. She had gone inside the building and
sprayed its walls with liquid concrete. When this had set, she
persuaded the workmen to knock away the outside walls of
the house and thus leave the concrete standing as a negative
of the interior. She had previously made similar moulds from
cupboards, baths and single rooms, but this was her first
house. The result she described as a 'statement about
Thatcherism' and a 'ghostly negative of reality'.

The structure was big and, when floodlit at night, undeniably impressive. As I was bid by the *Financial Times*, I
spent some moments pondering the 'quiet, spiritual, poetic'
qualities of the concrete, though I could have done that in
many places in the East End. I reflected on how the work
'exposed in a way no one has ever quite done before the
spaces which shape our lives'. Putting all thought of Vermeer
and Cézanne from my mind, I concentrated on the shapes.
Try as I did, their political and aesthetic message seemed
facile and banal. This was a mould, no more nor less.

Whiteread's house is what most people would regard as a
folly. Its antecedents if they are needed are not the paintings
of Turner but the structures that Pope and Walpole erected
in the gardens of their Thames-side residences. The house
must have taken its creator time and effort, but then so does
a grotto, and a grotto is for use. I could not see the point in
demolishing the house when the prizegiving was over. Follies,
even in neo-brutalist concrete, have their place, as might a
sense of the absurd in this part of London. But the locals
hated the eyesore and they had their rights. The building duly

came down. I cannot believe it will stand on the record as one of the major works of British art in the 1990s.

What I long to find is a language in which to speak to these artists that is other than nonsense. A new novel or play can be discussed by its critics in plain English. The glories of English grammar are available free of charge to any who wishes to explain his or her work to the public. I can go out into the street and argue whether the Booker judges have chosen the best work of fiction, or compare a play by Alan Bennett with one by Tom Stoppard. When a writer says his work reflects his love of Conrad or Faulkner, I know what these words mean. Yet when one of the Turner competitors paints crude stripes across a canvas and cites Conrad and Faulkner as his inspiration, I have no idea whether he is talking sense or rubbish. He has stripped words of their usefulness. The obscurantism suggests a collapse of the critical faculty, the faculty most sacred to art.

A number of London critics, notably those in the *Evening Standard* and *Spectator*, have taken the view that much of the work now being displayed in the Tate, the Hayward and the Serpentine galleries is the outcome of a cultural cul-de-sac. It is the product of Duchamp's blind alley, where 'I do not believe in art, only artists.' I agree. At the Tate Gallery I see visitors looking at lumps of steel or twisted rags and giggling with embarrassment. They are like tourists accosted by a three-card trickster. They cluster in relief round a video of the 'sculptors' at work. They see the video as the window that might explain the art. They treat the artist as the focus of their attention, not the art. (The judges take the same view in ensuring there is a woman on the Turner shortlist each year.)

Sceptics are always vulnerable to the charge that they are falling into the same trap as Ruskin did in his great fight with Whistler. They would have rejected Whistler's work as so much Jackson Pollock. They would have ridiculed his remark that 'art should be independent of all claptrap, should stand alone and appeal to the artistic sense of eye or ear'. Such conservative critics are accused of not recognizing progressive

185

genius. They reject art's role in upsetting, challenging and standing convention on its head. By all means admire the Old Contemptibles of nineteenth-century watercolour, say the modernists. They are easy. But do not dismiss modernism just because you cannot understand its language.

The conservative's reply is to say, in all honesty, that he is being conned. Ruskin may have been mistaken. But there is such a thing as a confidence trick in art. The Dadaists made a cult of it. Much modern poetry is not poetry but prose laid out oddly on the page. Much computer originated music is ingenious rather than beautiful and is near intolerable on the ear. In these cases, as in much of modern painting and sculpture, I do not sense any creative imagination at work. To call it art is to abuse language. I am not persuaded.

This is different from art that I happen not to like. I find the plays of Harold Pinter, the music of Stockhausen, the ballets of Béjart, often incomprehensible and usually shocking. The architecture of Norman Foster leaves me cold. But in these cases I am ready to acknowledge the presence of an artist. I feel a talent wrestling to carry T. S. Eliot's great tradition forward into new territory. Modernism will be, perhaps must be, hard. That is incontestable.

The critical faculty cannot be suspended merely because an art gallery such as the Tate asks to be 'taken seriously'. Indeed where such an Establishment appears to enjoy a monopoly of state patronage, criticism has a positive duty to be independent. We are not in the presence of Gombrich's art critic, so drunk that he cannot tell a friend from a lamp-post and so embraces both. We must be able to stand back and ask where Ruskin may have been at fault in attacking Whistler, and where he may have been right. The critical faculty applies the same standard to modern artists. But it must be able to debate. At the Academy we can compare Ruskin with Whistler. We can see the point of their argument. I can find no argument between true modern artists such as Hockney or Kitaj and those on show at the Hayward or the Tate. I simply cannot take the latter seriously.

24

MESSING ABOUT WITH GEORGE

THE BLOW when it came was almost too crude. For two episodes the titans of the BBC's drama department had kept the faith. *Middlemarch*, the glory of English fiction, was more than respected, it was enhanced. Here once again was a serial to make us rush home and watch. Television was back in real time. We were not prepared to wait for a video version. Literary integrity had remarried television drama after what seemed an eternity.

Then wham! The critical moment was that of Lydgate's proposal to the lovely Rosamund Vincy. The ambitious young doctor has been privately warned off her by her scheming relatives. He takes the warning to heart. She does not know, and is mortified by his neglect of her attentions. They meet, half by chance, alone in her drawing room. Tears well up in Rosamund's 'forget-me-not' eyes and Lydgate's resolve starts to crumble. This is George Eliot at her most sensitive. The tears were the 'crystallising feather-touch' that 'shook flirtation into love'. Lydgate moves towards Rosamund and takes her in his arms, gently as if she were a patient. He kisses each large tear. She is not angry, writes Eliot, 'but she moved backwards a little in timid happiness and Lydgate could now sit near her and speak more completely.' In half an hour they are engaged. The encounter is one of supreme tenderness. The blooming of young love has seldom been so exquisitely portrayed.

So what would the BBC make of this turning point in the drama? The corporation felt that Eliot made a total hash of it. It believed that what should have happened was this. Lydgate speaks the words and then charges across the room at the sight of Rosamund's tears. To swelling background music she sobs, 'I'm so unhappy if you do not care about me.' He seizes her in his arms and they subject each other to instant, jaw-crushing mouth-to-mouth resuscitation. *Middlemarch* gets a sudden dose of *Neighbours*.

As I reeled from the shock I began to tick off other liberties that this episode had taken with Eliot's novel. No, the novel does not say Dorothea was sexually rejected by her husband Casaubon in bed. The enigma of the relationship, perhaps of the whole book, is that Eliot specifically does not tell us this. We do not know on what rock their love foundered. To leave such things private is the novelist's privilege. No, Mary Garth does not give all her savings to the spendthrift Fred Vincy, with whom she is in love. She gives the money to her father Caleb Garth, whom she also loves, to pay Fred's debts. This division in affection is crucial to her character, and possibly to Eliot's also. Caleb Garth was based on her own father. No, the artist whom Dorothea encounters in Rome does not draw her surreptitiously, thus implying an early infidelity. He draws her with Casaubon's full permission.

What is the point of such senseless departures from the plot? Who, I wonder, dictates the censorship? The screenplay of the *Middlemarch* series is by Andrew Davies, a respected writer for television who would not wilfully abuse George Eliot's work. I can only assume that some higher executive, desperately watching the ratings and knowing the way of the world, must have hauled him in and told him that some of the scenes lacked a bit of you-know-what. 'Hey Davies,' he must have said in Sam Goldwyn style, 'get hold of that guy Eliot and tell him to jazz up the love scenes.' In which case, why not ask the writer simply to produce a period romance

set in a provincial English town and leave Eliot out of it? I
imagine the directors of the National Gallery could adjust
their Titians and Goyas to titillate modern taste and pull in
a few more visitors. The Royal Shakespeare Company could
beef up some of the bard's weaker lines, and the Carmen
Jones concept could be extended to all the operas of Puccini
and Verdi. On the whole, the custodians of the world's
masterpieces do not play fast and loose with them in this way.
Past theatre owners did indeed do this with Shakespeare –
notably by giving *King Lear* a happy ending. We deride
bowdlerization today. We respect the original. Why does film
feel free to tamper with a novel?

I suppose cinema was ever thus. There have been enough
adulterations of great works on television and film for the
viewer to have become thick-skinned about such liberties.
Normally television dramatization takes a work and plunders
it simply for a plot – plots are always hard to come by. Characterization is brought 'up to date' and complexity is usually
eliminated. This strips the original of its creative range.
Heroes are fitted to stereotypes. The result is an illustration
that rarely illumines the work, as for instance in the BBC's
recent travesty of Stendhal's *Scarlet and Black* or in many
attempts at *War and Peace*.

My purism is the more heartfelt over *Middlemarch* because
the dramatization is otherwise sound. The blemish is so
clearly a blemish, rather than a wholesale distortion. *Middlemarch* is as good as the BBC's immaculate Henry James adap-
tations or Granada's *Brideshead*. The casting is superb. Had
Eliot seen Robert Hardy's Mr Brooke she would surely have
banged the table and cried, 'That's him!' The BBC's Vincy,
Bulstrode, Lydgate and Chetham will from now on be welcome guests at my *Middlemarch* board. Not since Peggy Ash-
croft in *Jewel in the Crown* have I come across such attention
paid to accent as an indicator of the gradations of English
class.

The supporting cast is equally strong: the gossiping women,
the scheming governors of the hospital, the raucous market
traders. Some have criticized the number of horses, but they

were ubiquitous in nineteenth-century England. The architecture is wrong. Middlemarch was mercantile Warwickshire (whether Nuneaton or Coventry is a matter of debate) rather than honey-stoned Stamford. But the balance between people and context is controlled and Eliot's narrative energy is never dissipated.

The women in the piece are slightly less sure-footed, perhaps because Eliot seems to have been ambivalent towards them. One moment I feel she herself is Dorothea, Mary Garth, even Rosamund, the next she is the aloof commentator, observing them from a distance and even inserting her judgments into the text. Dorothea, the surface prim heroine and goody-two-shoes, is there to resolve the plot and release its victims from their bondage. She might at times have strayed into the play from a work by Dickens. Her appeal to the modern reader lies in her inner doubts and agonies. Eliot devotes to them pages of psychological analysis, but this cannot be communicated on the screen, however subtle the expressions on an actor's face. Perhaps the camera can never equal the written word as a conveyor of emotional complexity. Likewise Merchant Ivory could not master the stilted self-absorption of Stevens the butler in the film version of *The Remains of the Day*. Dorothea is at root the creature of a literary imagination. Nor did the BBC help her recreator, Juliet Aubrey, by portraying her husband, Casaubon, as almost an Addams Family ghoul. He was far more interesting than he is here. Eliot herself, when asked on whom he was based, replied that he was in part herself.

Despite their obvious differences, I have always regarded *Middlemarch* as England's *War and Peace*, epitomes of their respective countries and cultures at a turning point in the mid-nineteenth century. Both novels were written at the end of the 1860s and recalled upheavals of a generation earlier. Eliot and Tolstoy both used the clash of human personalities as a metaphor for a clash of class, culture and ideology. Both used subplots heavy with political messages – the advance of freemasonry or of electoral and medical reform – as battering rams against the élites of a pre-industrial society. Both set

190

the land, its seasons, its owners, its workers and their ancient ways, against modern history rushing past its gates – literally rushing in Tolstoy's account of Napoleon's march to and from Moscow.

Tolstoy's history was on a grander scale, the St Petersburg court and the manoeuvres of the French emperor back and forth across Europe. Eliot's history was more microscopic. The impact of political and professional change on a small Midlands town is no match for 1812. Yet the searches of Lydgate and of Pierre for self-fulfilment are not dissimilar, searches that took them through intense emotional barrenness on the way to life's final compromises. The figures of Fred Vincy and Nikolai Rostov have parallels, not least in finding fulfilment in the pleasure of estate management. Eliot studied the contrast of a town and its surrounding country, as Tolstoy was fascinated by the contrast of court and provincial estate. She set radical against conservative in each context, Brooke against Chetham in the country, Lydgate against his hospital tormentors in the town. She emerges as champion of the radicals, but only just. Neither Brooke nor Lydgate is permitted to realize his dreams. Both are humiliated.

As for the town versus country, Eliot is unashamedly country. The landed estate and its inheritances triumph. Dorothea bestows her largesse on all who wish it, foregoing it only when true love finds her out. (I share the view of most critics that the ending of *Middlemarch* is weak, as is that of *The Mill on the Floss*.) More to the point, the men of prosperity in the town are treated mercilessly. Old Vincy is the butt of constant ridicule and the great benefactor, Bulstrode, is cruelly brought low by malice and his past. Had he been Jewish, this would qualify as an anti-Semitic novel. It is certainly an anti-Dissenter one. The provincial towns of Victorian England were built on the philanthropy of men such as Bulstrode, yet George Eliot affects to despise them.

All interlopers find themselves on the wrong side of Eliot's pen. She rewards inherited wealth, unambitious labour and well-matched couples. She can do no better with Lydgate than punish him for his professional and marital pretensions

191

with exile to Bath. 'Confound their petty politics,' he cries in despair at his Middlemarch enemies, but their petty politics win in the end. The two champions of the 1832 Reform Act, Brooke and Ladislaw, both fail in their political ambitions. But both are permitted to recover their status, the one by being a gentleman, the other by being the object of Dorothea's love.

Television can still bring great works to life and great themes to mind. *Middlemarch* reintroduced me to old friends and set me worrying anew over their little agonies. But I would prefer it if George Eliot, rather than the BBC, were allowed to be arbiter of their fates.

25

GOOSE TERROR

I CAN spot a cover-up. The authorities recently announced that the starling had overtaken the sparrow as Britain's 'most seen' garden bird. So what? They added that magpies were becoming so numerous as to constitute an epidemic. We knew that. Then came the common seagull, and rumours that it might carry bubonic plague. These were pure scare tactics, a diversion. The true threat lay elsewhere and no amount of concealment would keep it from the British people.

Two years ago a friend of mine dug himself a lawn on a Dorset hillside. He lovingly levelled it, sowed it and began to mow. He installed drainage in the approved places, but apparently without success. After the first heavy downpour, he looked out of his window and saw, in the place of his lawn, a sizeable lake. Worse, in place of a garden alive with flora and fauna he had the ornithological equivalent of a rottweiler pen. *Branta canadensis* had come. The geese knew neither manners nor hygiene. They ate everything in sight, drove off every rival and, worse of all, excreted without ceasing.

Canada goose excretum, as every municipal park-keeper will attest through clenched teeth, is a lethal substance. Its inch-long pellets of green slime are revolting and toxic. A well-built goose will defecate every two or three minutes throughout the day. A flock can deposit a hundredweight in and round your pond in a week. No use has yet been found for the stuff, other than to burglar-proof crazy paving. But I am assured from Whitehall in all seriousness that 'an interdepartmental group is working on it'. Details of their deliberations are still secret.

As their name suggests Canada geese are native to North America. Each year they fly north for the summer in what is America's most poetic natural migration. Up the great 'flyways' they go – the east and west coast routes or the catchments of the Mississippi and Missouri rivers – to nest in the safety of the Canadian tundra. They fly back south for winter, at a stately 45 miles per hour. The Concorde-like profile of a *Branta canadensis* in flight, with its grey-white body, black head and snowy white bib, has made it the connoisseur's bird. Sir Peter Scott called the congregations of these geese in the shallows of a lake 'the finest wildlife spectacle still to be seen'.

Canadas belong to these gigantic spaces. They are the supertankers of the aerial ocean, gracefully cruising the skies, their soft honking call echoing from afar. The birds are alien to Britain. They were first brought by Charles II for his menagerie in St James's Park, where they remain in embarrassingly large numbers. British Canadas do not migrate. They stay put and grow fat, and familiarity breeds nuisance. A pair of geese is fertile for a decade. It can produce half a dozen goslings a year and is completely monogamous. Mating is for life. The Canada multiplies fast because it is so protective of its young. Neither parent strays from the nest during incubation and a mother will not hesitate to attack any predator, including foxes and humans. The ornithologist Kit Howard Breen records one desperate assault on two women who had inadvertently strayed near a nest. The attack included landing on their shoulders, beaks tearing at their hair.

The resident population in Britain has risen from a reported 2,000 at the end of the last war to more than 60,000 now. This is probably an under-estimate. Numbers are expected to double every eight years. These geese pollute water supplies, parks, golf courses and beaches. In America, the town of Stoneham, Massachusetts was attacked in 1988 by thousands of geese, who stripped it of every blade of grass. In Connecticut geese have forced the closure of shellfish beds, undeterred by electric fences, scarers and birdshot. Whether or not they prey on other birds is a subject hotly debated between the bird's admirers and its critics. Canadas certainly leave little room or food for other species. All that two geese need is a stretch of water and an adjacent park or cornfield and they will settle in and breed without ceasing. There is no nonsense about taking off north for the summer.

Americans are permitted to hunt Canada geese and have in the past come near to wiping them out over whole areas of North America. Hunting is now more tightly controlled, too tightly for the peace of mind of some farmers. In Britain goose hunting is permitted in the winter months. But a hunter is ill-advised to tell polite society he is off to shoot Canada geese. It is the shortest route to ostracism. Wandsworth Council in London found itself host to 200 Canadas in Battersea Park in 1993. It ordered their destruction as pests and the contract went to Rentokil. Within hours of this news becoming public, crowds of citizens led by the ubiquitous 'actresses and writers' descended on the park to protect the creatures. The council soon realized Wandsworth was to be no Hamelin. The geese might be pests to some but not to others. The pied pipers from Rentokil declined to proceed with the cull, fearing for their public image. The Canadas remain.

Even the magazine *Country Life* has felt obliged to enter the fray on the side of the authorities. It dubbed the birds the 'thugs of the bird kingdom'. The conservationist writer, Geoffrey Lean, catalogued the frantic measures being taken behind the scenes to meet an infestation he described as out of control. In July, the Environment Department had sent marksmen to St James's Park at dawn where they had shot no fewer than 100 Canadas. This had been done in total secrecy and with silencers fixed to their guns.

Others employed less drastic, or at least more cunning,

measures. Some local councils were pricking goose eggs. Others were coating them with paraffin. Milton Keynes, where every avenue is interlaced with tastefully landscaped lakes, was at its wits' end. Council officials had taken to stealing goose eggs, hard-boiling them in mobile tea urns and returning them to nests so that the mother geese would not realize something was amiss and lay new ones. This was regarded as a harsh trick to play on a creature known for its maternal instinct. A terrified spokesman for Milton Keynes Council refused to elaborate on the matter. Methods employed to eradicate Canada geese are the nearest British local government has to a state secret.

The British are at their most hilarious when heart and head are in conflict. One man's romantic wanderer of the skies is another's feathered vermin. What glides in balletic formation across one lake, fouls the banks of another. Those accepting the need for quick remedial action also cry, 'There must be another way'. The friends of the Canada goose know that they have emotion on their side, but the enemies know it too. Deep within Whitehall's Environment Department is a 'Canada goose working group' seeking a cure to the plague that does not incur adverse publicity. I see them making their way to a basement bunker, having told their secretaries they were 'popping out to the shop'. The door is locked. No minutes are taken, nor is any decision. I understand that at one recent meeting the group merely passed the buck to the Central Scientific Laboratory, asking for 'more research into the goose's aggressive behaviour'. I imagine the lab was told to take its time.

Whitehall is still smarting from the affair of the Ruddy Duck. This duck, like the goose, is an extraneous species imported into Britain by Sir Peter Scott in the 1950s. The birds escaped from his bird sanctuary and swiftly multiplied to 3,500 pairs. These enterprising creatures made their way across the Channel into France. From there they followed the path of Don Giovanni into Spain where they were delighted to discover the lovely and timid Spanish White-headed Duck. The result was species gang rape and an appeal by the Spanish government to the European Community. The ethnic purity of the White-headed Duck was at risk. Ornithological gene pollution is apparently against some law and the Spanish were appalled. Whether or not the White-headed had any choice in the matter, it was unable to resist the advances of the Ruddy. The Spanish duck was soon on the way to 'hybridization' and endangered species status. Madrid has appealed to London to have the Ruddy Duck expelled back to North America. Presumably all surviving Ruddys would have to experience the genocide practised by the Environment Department on the Canada geese. Britain was reported to be 'studying its response' to the Madrid demand. Nobody knows what to do. There are dark mutterings about the survival of the fittest.

Massacring 60,000 wild geese, or even repatriating them to America, over the bodies of screaming actresses is the last thing the British government needs to contemplate. I doubt if officials have even brought this horror to Downing Street's attention. The Royal Society for the Protection of Birds is stunned into statesmanship on the subject. Strident in defence of all things feathered, it mumbles and stutters when bird is pitted against bird. Careful not to appear anti-goose, its spokesmen have none the less to be sympathetic to the outrage felt by farmers and gardeners. They point out that wild geese can be shot in the winter hunting season, and even out of season where the licensing authorities issue a special pest permit. The society was not opposed to this limited culling, 'but we are against shooting to reduce the overall goose population without evidence that these birds are aggressive to other wildfowl'. In other words the buck was again being passed to 'further research'.

The goose conundrum is similar to many arguments over the balance of Britain's natural history. The Canada is not a native. Like the rhododendron, the grey squirrel and countless human imports, these creatures are newcomers that flourish in competition with apparently weaker natives. The world is for the strong. But birds are special. They contribute to the ecological balance and need our protection. The immigration authorities do not know what to do. The ornithologists are reluctant to tell them.

The wild goose has a beauty and grace of movement that gives it 'charismatic species' status. It is the dolphin of the sky. Exterminate a starling or a pigeon by all means, but a local council boils a goose egg at its peril. Goodness knows where this will end. Every means of limiting the goose population or deterring flocks from particular locations has failed. These are the world's most determined guests. Something will have to be done. But I would be sorry to see the birds depart altogether. The great skeins of geese moving across the sky, wings beating in unison, grouping and regrouping in V-formation, offer the most majestic of aerial ballets. They are nature's creation and are beautiful. As such they deserve our conservation. They should at least be persuaded to migrate north for the summer. Perhaps we should all learn to love goose pâté.

26

DO YOU SPEAK WINE?

HERE WAS an item of news that stopped me in mid-slurp. The editors of that no-nonsense periodical *Which? Wine Guide* estimate that one in twelve wine corks may be faulty. This means that one in twelve bottles of wine is likely to have been contaminated by contact with air. This in turn implies that when we nervously taste the morsel poured out for us by the wine waiter – if the wine is really off he should take it back even after a full glass – we ought to question one glass in twelve. But as the editors of the guide conclude, British customers are so insecure in their senses and wine merchants so patronizing that few people ever go back to complain of corked or oxidized wine. If they taste bad wine, they simply buy less of it. *Which?* would like to see more 'aggression' by customers and more wine tasting by off-licence staff.

I can think of no surer route to violence: irate customers who have downed a bottle of Bulgarian cabernet fighting with shop assistants deep in a back-room tasting session. The best hope is what happened to me once in a wine shop in Connecticut. I had asked for a Burgundy. The merchant said he had a case but was not sure if it was still 'up to it'. He suggested we open one bottle to see. It seemed fine to me, but he was eager to display his knowledge of its inadequacy. Eventually

I insisted on buying a bottle, despite his reservations. We compromised with me paying half-price.

I am convinced that the real cause of insecurity among wine-drinkers is that those promoting and selling wine no longer speak English. They speak wine. When Woody Allen asked his question of the waiter, 'Do you speak shellfish?' he might equally have asked 'Do you talk winespeak or is there an interpreter present?' I assume wine-sellers like to keep it that way.

I have a private collection of winespeak. It began long ago after a visit to a Berni Inn steakhouse. The wine list was tabloid. Three white wines were on offer, described simply as, 'Mâcon, dry; Sauternes, sweet; Chablis, roughly in between.' No description can equal this for clarity and economy of meaning. To most customers of Berni Inns, this is as much as they could want to know about their wine, no more, no less. All else would have been showing off by the proprietor. My finest exhibit is for a red wine produced by that august institution, the Tanzanian State Milling Corporation. It was called Dodoma. 'Try a glass,' said the menu. 'It is as subtle as a charging rhino.' Nobody could be in any doubt there.

Modern winespeak is devoid of such helpful simplicity. What was once a jargon for communicating among specialists has become a scrambled pidgin. Most grammar books warn the writer of English off the use of adjectives. Nouns and verbs, they say, should bear the burden of description. Winespeak's adjectives burst from the bottle like shaken champagne. Banana-ey, chocolatey, forward, spicy, autumnal and coquettish are regularly in use. Fragments of this language litter newspaper wine columns and the menus of country house hotels. They are meaningless to the layman, and I imagine they are to most of those who write them. Winespeak is the nearest English comes to gibberish. But I have longed for a complete text, a tract which philologists could deconstruct, a Rosetta stone of this parlance. Recently I discovered one. I felt like Howard Carter at the door of Tutankhamun's tomb.

The venue was the restaurant car of a British Rail express out of King's Cross. Our journey was not going well. 'Severe delays' were announced and we soon halted in the middle of a field of fenland corn. 'Vandals have brought down the line between Huntingdon and Grantham,' came the announce-ment. As compensation we were offered a discount on our ticket and a free drink on British Rail. I picked up the wine list and read as follows (spelling and punctuation retained):

The InterCity wine list reflects the reality of today's ultra-modern railway, intent upon efficiency, speed and punctuality, with high-speed trains spearing effortlessly through the countryside, I therefore wanted our wines to be modern too.

Hardy's Nottage Hill Chardonnay: soft, ripe . . . light enough to quench your thirst but with a delicious taste of apricots and cloves to keep you wanting more.

Hardy's Nottage Hill Cabernet Sauvignon: another Aussie stunner – loads of colour, loads of flavour, but the flavour is soft, not rasping, and the fruit is deep plums and blackcurrants with just a hint of spice.

Sauvignon de Touraine: pale, bone dry, as crisp as a green apple, as fresh as country nettles and meadow grass.

Chardonnay, Vin de Pays d'Oc: stunning Chardonnay . . . It has a deep, nutty, toasty intensity that the best white Burgundies would be proud of.

Barossa Valley Australian Chardonnay: If you've never tried the true show-stopping, ultra-ripe, honeyed nutty style of an Australian Chardonnay at full throttle, settle back in your seat, check that the next station isn't yours and give yourself a blast of this Down Under Wonder.

Beaujolais Villages, Georges Duboeuf: It's the sheer bright, breezy gluggability of this wine that attracted us,

201

with its fresh flavour of bananas and strawberry and a sprinkling of pepper to whet your appetite.

Crozes Hermitage Rouge: Fabulous deep, hearty red from France's Rhone Valley. It's a real mouthfiller, but don't be nervous – the flavour is all chocolate and plums and blackberries finished off with cream.

At first glance this appears to be mere drivel, the ravings of a copywriter unsure how to fill space on his wine list. No rail traveller could possibly find any guidance to what he might or might not be drinking in such language. It defies even Thurber's famous satire, 'a naïve domestic Burgundy without any breeding'. Such phrases had a certain class, as illustrated by Ronald Searle's cartoon of a 'delicate bouquet', with flowers erupting from the rim of the taster's glass. The British Rail wine list by contrast is crude, rugby club talk, 'sheer gluggability' or 'blast of Down Under Wonder'. Its execrable grammar and punctuation might serve as a GCSE horror question. I had the temerity to ask the stewardess if she could help with a translation of any of the entries on her list. She replied hesitantly but with commendable clarity, 'I think it simply means they're nice.'

I fully realize that this language is not meant to describe the wine. It is meant to sell it. Words drift upwards from the page like helium-filled balloons with slogans on them. Nobody is asking, 'Would sir prefer a wine tasting of bananas, strawberries and pepper to one tasting of apples, nettles and grass, or even one tasting of chocolate, plum, blackberry and cream?' Nobody on board the 12.00 from King's Cross could speak wine. No interpreter was present. There was no clue as to what the list was about, despite its not inconsiderable price. The author of the list, Mr Oz Clarke, was not around to help.

How such phrases appear to those for whom wine is not a professional pursuit is a mystery beyond solution. The task of putting taste, the most subjective of the senses, into words and then words into price is something that has long vexed the wine trade. Ancient writers on wine did not bother. From Galen to Rabelais and Montaigne, wine was good or bad, appreciated for what it was and where it was from rather than for what nuances of taste could be detected by one drinker or another. Falstaff went no further than to call his beloved sack 'a marvellous searching wine' that 'perfumes the blood'.

By the nineteenth century, wine experts were joining doctors and lawyers in developing a jargon to shield them from the common man. To declare 'I just don't like it' of a great wine was not permissible. As the curator said to the American tourist who professed a dislike for Rembrandt, 'It is not Rembrandt that is on trial, sir, it is you.' Wine is not to be enjoyed or avoided, like food. You might like or dislike pâté de fois gras or oysters without anybody holding it against you. But a great wine is not open to argument. It is to be approached with reverence, like music or architecture.

In his treatise on the art of wine-tasting, Émile Peynaud utters a cry of frustration at being forced to put into words what he has just tasted. The multitudinous sensations that assail the tongue and the olfactory nerves at the back of the nose are complex and intimate. No language can do them justice. 'Yet,' he says wisely, 'to know is to be able to name.' And to name requires a vocabulary. Peynaud lists 200 different words to describe just the appearance of a wine, let alone its taste. Michael Broadbent, in his admirable pocket guide to wine-tasting, lists 120 common words used of the flavour of a wine, but has 12 pages of more esoteric ones. He admits to having been shaken to discover that two professional colleagues made contradictory statements about identical wines at a wine-tasting. He concluded that if professionals could disagree 'on whether a wine was full, light or dry, or whatever, it was less likely a sensory problem then a semantic one'.

Mr Broadbent's list is mostly beyond me. It includes vegetal, twiggy, stewed, mawkish, beefy, goaty and sweaty saddle. None of these could apply to any liquid that has passed my lips, except perhaps soup. He does not include Mr Clarke's gluggability, toasty or country nettle. He tackles both honeyed and nutty, but not in terms that could possibly be used of the same wine at the same time. As for a Rhône being a 'mouthfiller' cocktail of chocolate, plum, blackberry and cream, rail passengers must await the winespeak equivalent of the decipherment of Linear B.

What are we left with? Mr Clarke is using words to paint marketing pictures. His pictures are not so much Monet as Jackson Pollock. He hopes that by slapping a dozen colours onto the page in what I take to be the imagery of Essex man, he can stimulate the saliva glands of passengers. Presumably the technique works. But the language is the degeneration of a coterie jargon, invented and codified to put into words what is inherently indescribable, the experience of smell.

The four tastes of the tongue, salt, sweet, acid and bitter, are enough to tell us whether a wine is adulterated or gone sour. They are the nearest wine-tasting can get to fact. To go farther is to enter a realm in which words are drained of their normal content. It is inconceivable that when one wine expert says that a Burgundy reminds him of chocolate and another that it reminds him of blackberries and cream, they can possibly be conveying sense to each other. Such statements are not like aesthetic judgments, where the viewer of a picture can at least refer to the details of the paint or the likeness of a portrait or the shading of colour. Broadbent says that a lecturer on wine must 'select words which are evocative and meaningful and use words which can be clearly related to the wine being tasted'. He seems to separate what is factual from what is fanciful. It is, he says, 'better to fumble and stumble than not to try to express ourselves at all'.

My problem is that I do not see how the words offered to describe the flavour of wine can be other than fanciful. They are language as metaphor, and elusive metaphor at that. I presume that those who taste vast quantities of wine come to know the special characteristics of individual vinyards and vintages. Even then I am genuinely puzzled as to how they can discuss these characteristics with each other, except in the most pretentious terms. The difficulty for the layman is that the private codes shared by the professionals use words that have specific meaning in the real world, 'chocolate-ey' for instance. This makes winespeak doubly mystifying. I would almost prefer the professionals to speak Esperanto or some artificial tongue. I regard these professionals as poets of the senses. They are choosing words to express not wine but their own sensations on drinking wine. When André Simon described a Chablis as having the 'grace of a silver willow' he was painting a word picture reflecting his own state of mind. He conveys no facts about the wine. Majestic prose poems may be stimulated by wine. The language of wine is the imagery of human experience not the imagery of fermented grape juice. The BR wine list was merely dreadful poetry.

The best way to demystify wine, and ultimately get more people to buy and enjoy it, is to leave winespeak to the coterie and not inflict it on the consumer. The use of winespeak in journalism and menu-writing is the most off-putting of all linguistic snobbery. Let the experts tell us what is in a bottle of wine – that is all we expect of a food writer – and leave us to make up our own mind how much we enjoy it and what metaphors best describe it to us. 'Come,' said Falstaff, 'good wine is a good familiar creature if it be well used. Exclaim no more against it.' Neither exclaim too much in its favour. Good wine and good English do not mix.

27

VIVAT UMBRIA

I PREFER geography's underdogs. I like the little places. I prefer Provence to the Côte d'Azur, the River Lot to the Dordogne, Bruges to Amsterdam. Above all I prefer Umbria to Tuscany. I will concede the whole Florentine canon. Tuscany can count its triumphs, from Duccio to Piero, from Donatello's Baptistry doors and Siena's campo, from *bistecca alla fiorentina* to *chianti classico*. But no longer can we dissociate places from the people that have become part of them. Tourists become a feature of the sites they wish to see. A landscape is its tenantry. Tuscany's immense popularity may be justified, but that popularity renders it the less attractive. Today the Gloucestershire *condottieri* (and their German and Dutch equivalents) descend on the place each summer, straw-hatted astride their steel-clad Volvos. They seize villa after villa and give no quarter. They behave as if they owned the place, and many of them do. So I concede Florence, Pisa, Siena and San Gimignano and fall back like Fabius south of Lake Trasimene. There I draw a line from Orvieto to Perugia and make my stand. Here Chiantishire shall not pass.

Tuscany boasts that it was the cradle of the Renaissance, but Umbria was its conception and genesis. Long before that, Umbria was the beginning of Italy. Here were the first settlements of farming people west of the Aegean. Here the early Romans made their earliest and most lasting conquest. Here were the Sabine women. Umbria was home to two of Europe's oldest known languages, Umbrian and Etruscan. It was the landscape beloved of Virgil and was thus the first landscape on record to offer aesthetic pleasure rather than just hard work. 'Fortunate is the man', said Virgil, 'who has come to know the gods of the countryside.' Scrape the surface of any Umbrian hill or meadow and you will scrape at three millennia of human activity. No place on earth has handed down to us so much antiquity so little altered by time.

Umbria is for the most part higher and greener than Tuscany. Despite being more southerly it is cooler. Its fields have more diverse crops, its hills seem more intimate, except beyond Spoleto where the wild Marches begin. A Tuscan wood seems to be of one species of tree. An Umbrian wood is pine mixed with poplar, oak, lime, ash, olive. The rolling landscape from Todi to Terni could, after an occasional shower of spring rain, pass for Herefordshire. Evening light falls across the contours in the greys and blues of Perugino and Pinturicchio. The climate itself is Umbrian school, softening the edges of hills with valley mist.

Robert Browning, seeking to be 'alone with my soul', found Florence already overcrowded in the last century. Today he would regard all Tuscany as intolerable, unless like so many British migrants he ruminated by his villa swimming pool all day. Florence and Pisa are under permanent siege. The road south to Siena is thick with foreign number plates. These cities are claimed as the property not of Tuscany, not even of Italy, but of the world. The villa boom is doing to the slopes of Chianti what a similar boom did 20 years ago to the once-lovely hills behind Nice. It is suburbanizing and internationalizing them. Umbria by comparison is still Italian. Prices are lower. English cars and newspapers are rareties. I am under no illusion that this will last. So *carpe diem*, seize the day.

I find it impossible to choose a favourite between Umbria's five great towns, Perugia, Orvieto, Assisi, Gubbio and

Spoleto. They are each different yet equally compelling. They all contrive to be medieval in layout and architecture and yet wholly alive. Residence is not confined to the old or the weekender. Citizens live and work behind ancient walls in homes modernized without damage to the streetscape. Most houses are accessible only on foot. Historic streets have been defended against car-borne tourism by excluding all but resident traffic, a technique no English town has yet had the courage to employ. Perugia buries its cars beneath its great acropolis rock and carries visitors up underground escalators to the old Corso. Assisi absorbs two million pilgrims a year with scarcely a blemish on its thirteenth-century face.

There is about these towns a sense not of a distant past but of a sane future. They defy all those who said that modern cities must be adapted to the motor car or they will die. They declare the opposite. Cities must not be so adapted or they will indeed die. Modern citizens do not want to use motorized transport to get from home to work or play unless the planning of a city demands it of them. We would all prefer to walk if we could. In Umbria citizens seem at peace with their towns. Modern plumbing and telecommunication coupled with an espresso in the piazza offers anything that twentieth-century Milton Keynes could afford – and much more besides.

Yet this is not the whole of it. Umbria's achievement is to express, in village, town, church and fresco, the spirit of one of the great moments in civilization. The Franciscan Reformation began Europe's long unsteady march out of medieval mysticism. It was in the early 1200s, a century before Dante and Petrarch, three centuries before Erasmus, that the elusive figure of St Francis emerged from the clan strife of Assisi. He took hold of a culture locked in the gloom of Byzantium and the terrors of Norman mythology and taught it to conjugate the verb 'to love'. Why St Francis is so little noticed in Britain compared with the stars of the Renaissance is a puzzle. Perhaps his Catholic humanism never attracted northern Europeans as did the neo-classical rationalism of Florence and Rome. Perhaps he was just an

Umbrian. But had he not been an Umbrian he would not have been St Francis.

St Francis was the son of a much-travelled merchant and a Provençal mother. He was a 'new European' even at his birth in 1182. He spoke two or three languages. Prior to his conversion and marriage to 'Lady Poverty' he was man-about-town, soldier and troubadour, singing in the language of song, his mother's Provençal. The origins of his distinctive theology remain a mystery, as does his poignant relationship with Assisi's other patron, St Clara, founder of the Poor Clares. Yet the Franciscan balance between contemplative solitude and worldly commitment has kept its appeal down the centuries. To a Roman Church steeped in the pagan theology of fear, St Francis brought not just the duties of poverty, chastity and obedience; he offered new eyes through which to see human personality and the natural world as twin sources of joy. He restored to Christianity the Pauline emphasis on love.

This message, then so radical, coats the walls of the astonishing shrine at Assisi. The building ranks among the wonders of European art. On the death of St Francis, such was the cult already surrounding him that the fathers of the Roman Church chose discretion as the better part of valour. There was no beating Franciscanism: they had better join it. They permitted the Franciscans a more drastic break with convention than anything yet seen in Italy, more radical than anything Florence later dared. Along with the theology of the early church, the forms of Byzantine art were cast aside. Painters were invited to express a more plastic humanism. In Cimabue's fresco of the Crucifixion in the transept of the upper basilica, Mary Magdalene throws her arms skywards in a gesture of despair. We are lifted from centuries of immobility, from those staring Duccios in the Siena gallery, and hurled straight towards Picasso's *Demoiselles d'Avignon*.

Giotto's frescos of the life of St Francis portray for the first time in art (at least since classical times) human beings talking, arguing, grieving, loving and playing. Here also by Giotto is said to be the first portrait, the face of an Assisi noble painted direct on to a chapel wall. Most remarkable of all is that we can gaze at a 700-year-old fresco of St Francis himself, standing in the Piazza del Commune, then walk up the street and see the same piazza, the same houses and the same Roman Temple of Minerva.

The postwar revival of the St Francis cult is easy to understand. St Francis's teaching of meditation, peace and love appealed to the young of the 1960s and has not lost its appeal to their children. It combines gaiety with a certain fatalism. To some it is compatible with Buddhism and Hinduism. The famous *Canticle of the Creatures* became an anthem of the Greens in the 1970s. That Margaret Thatcher should have quoted such a free-thinking drop-out on the steps of Downing Street in 1979 was bizarre. But such is the range of his audience.

In his pre-war biography of St Francis, the Italian historian Corrado Ricci wrote that 'to understand a great man's mind, it is profitable to know the country of his choice: few things can so truly reveal his feelings.' Even those who do not follow the teachings of St Francis can understand them better in the serene Umbrian landscape. Here is the origin of their power. The saint's 'beloved vale of Spoleto' runs from Assisi up the valley of the Tiber through the Roman settlements of Spello, Bevagna and Montefalco to Spoleto itself. It must be virtually as he left it. The hill villages and towns hold their ancient profiles against the horizon, even if suburban fat has grown round their chins. Only the mechanism of modern agriculture intrudes, and perhaps farm reform will soon dispose of that. I imagine this country is safe for ever.

Traces of a culture stretching continuous through time are precious. I can gaze on the fields of Waterloo but sense little of Wellington's battle. I can linger in the piazzas of Florence but not spy the Medicis. The gilded barges of Tudor monarchs no longer flit up the Thames at Richmond, much as I try to bring them to my imagination. But I defy anyone to walk through the lanes of Assisi or the fields of Umbria and not feel that amiable friar chatting at his side, greeting a passing child or pointing to a rare bird. Here is a prophet truly honoured in his own house and country. Here is Europe's past at peace with its present – and I hope with its future.

The effort of uttering this first birth-cry of the Renaissance left Umbria exhausted. The region ossified and became poor. It never found the resources or the self-confidence to destroy its monuments or rebuild its cities and towns. All subsequent reformations, revivals and risorgimentos passed it by. Umbria remained true to St Francis. What a mercy. God save Umbria.

28

CLIMBING THE MATTERHORN

THE MATTERHORN is a dangerous mountain. It must have killed more people than any other mountain on earth, including Everest. From the memorials in the adjacent Alpine town of Zermatt to the trail up the mountain itself, its approaches are lined with the graves of those who trifled with it. The bureaucracies of Europe have yet to tame the Matterhorn with safety precautions. To experienced climbers the peak is no particular challenge except in poor weather. But its appeal is to the romantic amateur. I went to Zermatt to see how far an ordinary hill walker could sensibly get without equipment. The answer is half-way up and certainly no farther. Sheer terror got the better of me. But at least it was sheer terror that stopped me. As I turned back on the bluff a hundred feet above the Hörnli hut, I offered a vote of thanks to the fact that here at least I was permitted to risk my life without somebody telling me not to.

The challenge of the Matterhorn needs little explanation. Anybody who has stood in the main square of Zermatt will know it. Most of the world's great peaks require a trek even to their lowest slopes. The top is often not visible until the final assault. The Matterhorn's elongated pyramid soars over Zermatt, taunting any mountaineer to do battle the moment he arrives in town. There are no foothills. A cable car leads directly onto the main slope. To those who have come far and trained hard, the peak sneers at any postponement. Its customary cloud cap sneers as well. I have known climbers in the Monte Rosa Hotel driven to distraction as they watch the cloud clear from the peak then close in again just as they were setting off. The Matterhorn is a maddening tease.

The best antidote to recklessness is to visit the tiny Matterhorn museum and the adjacent English church, tucked under the cliff behind the hotel. Both are filled with monuments to Alpinists, most of them British, worsted in combat with the mountain. Here is a frayed rope, here a boot that slipped, here a picture of a heroic guide dragged to his death. The Matterhorn was the scene of surely the world's most famous mountaineering disaster, when Edward Whymper made the first successful conquest of the summit in 1865. It was the nineteenth recorded attempt and Whymper lost four of his party on the descent. A rope broke and three Englishmen and a Swiss guide fell to their deaths. Whymper, described as a 'cold and calculating mountaineer', never recovered from the subsequent enquiry, which followed unsubstantiated rumours that the three survivors had cut the rope by which the four were dangling. There were calls in Britain for Alpine mountaineering to be banned as too dangerous. Whymper did not climb the Matterhorn again for ten years. By then it was the ambition of every Alpinist. The first woman on the peak was also English, Lucy Walker in 1871.

The proper procedure for climbing the Matterhorn today is to hire a guide through the Swiss Mountain Club in the centre of the town. At £200 a day guides do not come cheap and will not take inexperienced strangers to the summit without at least a week of practice on a lesser peak. Every year takes its toll and in 1987 the Zermatt Alps claimed 28 deaths in just six weeks. The guides want some evidence of fitness and proficiency. Since the peak is often cloud-covered and a night in the Hörnli hut is normal before an early morning ascent, a commitment of time and money is required. I was surprised to see in a 1912 Baedeker that the Matterhorn was described as 'not of unusual difficulty or danger: climbing irons useful'. There are some fixed ropes now, though the lower ones I saw looked uncomfortably like the tragic relics in the Zermatt museum. I accepted early in my visit that I was not likely to reach the top at a first attempt. The Alpine Club could be relieved of responsibility for me.

Zermatt has long been the capital of British Alpinism. Its best-known hotel, the Monte Rosa, is filled with Victorian photographs of lords and ladies and their local guides in heroic poses against a Matterhorn backdrop. In winter the town is just another ski resort. Its streets are filled with those who delight not in reaching the tops of these mountains but in coming down them from half-way up. The appeal of skiing has always eluded me. In its cause the Zermatt authorities have defaced their slopes with concrete blockhouses, cables, pylons and trees cut to look like Forestry Commission spruce plantations. Skiing demands a charmless environment.

In summer, Zermatt reverses its geometry. Gentle paths rise through fields of flowers towards the snow line and the peaks. This is the time for an invasion of 'serious' walkers, Britons, Germans, French and Swiss, all treating the mountains as challenges not to technology but to thigh muscles. Alpine walkers once gloried in the loneliness of these mountains. Not any more. Zermatt has 108 hotels and sits at the centre of a cobweb of lifts and cable cars stretching north, south, east and west. But the peaks keep their isolation and their danger. They are above the ski line and none of those round Zermatt has yet suffered the indignity of a cable car and cafeteria at or close to the summit, as at Mount Pilatus or Mont Blanc.

When Mark Twain visited Zermatt in 1878, the mountains were already teeming with climbers following in Whymper's footsteps. Hundreds arrived each year, with the British Alpine Club at their social apogee. To the Swiss, these mountains were old familiars. They were not a test of imperial virility. Twain reacted much the same. His response to the sight of these athletic tourists was his satirical essay, *Climbing the Riffelberg*. The Riffelberg is a modest peak to the south-east of the town crowned (as in Twain's day) by a large nine-teenth-century hotel. Its chief distinction is that early Bronze Age artefacts were discovered on the Riffelhorn overlooking it, thus enabling the *Guinness Book of Records* to claim their makers as the first mountaineers.

Twain's suggested party for the conquest of this peak comprised no fewer than 198 persons. They included four surgeons, three chaplains, four pastry cooks, 44 muleteers, a botanist and a 'Latinist'. His team of guides cunningly found their way up by tracing the lines of tourists coming down. When he reached the top he was gratified to be greeted with rounds of applause from the assembled hotel guests. His proposed descent involved parachuting his entire party by umbrella onto the Gornergrat glacier, which sweeps beneath Monte Rosa opposite the Matterhorn. He was furious to find that his guides had forgotten the relevant Bradshaw, and thus lacked any information on the glacier's expected time of arrival back in Zermatt. This was finally calculated as being in the summer of AD 2378, or in Twain's irate words 'slower than the Ephesus to Smyrna railway'. He and his colleagues agreed that this was another case of European management incompetence. Had the glacier been in the hands of American private enterprise, it would have got them home in no time.

My own party owed more to Eric Newby than Mark Twain. Our gallant band of smokers, drinkers and the unfit set out with alpenstocks to see how far we would get. The sun was bright as we left the cable car station, though the air was alarmingly thin. The most disconcerting aspect of the early climb was to be stopping constantly for breath as large parties of Swiss pensioners trotted past carrying heavy rucksacks. At the famous rallying point for the final assault, the Hörnli hut at 3,260m, we collapsed over huge mugs of beer and plates of *rösti*. The peak soared 1,000 metres overhead, the wind dabbing it with fluffs of cloud.

Above Hörnli the going is altogether tougher. We encountered snow. The path is deserted, the air thins, the heart pumps and the Matterhorn takes on a different aura, black and menacing and certainly not for the casual tourist. The clouds seem to have a life of their own as they dash this way and that across the twisted faces of the peak. Prevailing winds have no meaning here, as many who thought they would hang-glide down the Matterhorn have found to their cost. A cross near a statue of the Madonna marks the spot where an American boy met his death. It was placed by his parents pleading with non-mountaineers to go no farther. As I read it, two German climbers encased in equipment came hurrying out of the mist above, silent as if pursued by ghosts. To my right lay the sheer drop of the northern glacier, where Whymper's party met its fate. I had reached my risk threshold. After the first two fixed ropes, I turned back.

There have been countless proposals to make my passage upwards easier, and thus ruin the Matterhorn. Even before Whymper's conquest, when the peak was thought unclimbable, a Swiss engineer proposed a road into the mountain and a spiral tunnel up inside it. He offered windows at various points so pedestrians could look out. In 1892 a railway was projected, first rack and pinion then funicular to the summit, where a terrace and restaurant would be built. A similar project was implemented on the adjacent Gornergrat summit, where Europe's highest hotel is open to all who can resist the altitude sickness. As recently as 1988 there was a proposal to floodlight the Matterhorn, covering its slopes with cables and lighting equipment.

All such ideas have so far been resisted. Nor has there been any safety directive demanding that the hard climbs be flattened to reduce accidents, though the fixed ropes and chain bridges on the lower slopes must leave the authorities open to challenge should they fall into disrepair. Even above Hörnli there is no barrier or other warning limiting access to experienced climbers. There are no railings, signs or legal disclaimers of responsibility. American negligence lawyers are not crouching behind every rock, offering to sue the Swiss government for any twisted ankle. The Matterhorn remains a thundering great risk.

Most nations dreadfully abuse their mountain tops. The highest peak in England and Wales, Snowdon, has a railway running to its summit. Other mountains throughout Europe have belvederes, radio stations and military bases ruining their solitude and usually their appearance. Britain's defence ministry cannot resist capping most peaks with a forest of masts and aerials. Yet the 4,000-metre peaks of the Alps defy all attempts to tame them. They are Switzerland's answer to those who might belittle it as a weak or diminutive state. They are nature's champions. Each year somebody picks up the gauntlet and loses. But the Swiss keep their regulators and safety inspectors at bay. We can hurl ourselves at the Matterhorn, test our strength, risk life and limb and experience the exhilaration of conquest. We are free to make up our own minds when to accept defeat. I admitted it with pleasure. But next time . . .

29

THE THREATENED
TROUBADOUR

I hear the nightingale,
That from the little blackthorn spinney steals
To the old hazel hedge that skirts the vale,
And still unseen sings sweet. The ploughman feels
The thrilling music as he goes along,
And imitates and listens; while the fields
Lose all their paths in dusk to lead him wrong,
Still sings the nightingale her soft melodious song.

I HAVE been given a book so delightful I cannot keep it to
myself. The book is about nightingales, just 100 pages long
and full of the same darting rhythms as that elusive bird.
Richard Mabey's *Whistling in the Dark* is poetry and prose,
natural history, memoir, myth, music and conservationist
tract. Every nightingale that has captivated the human
imagination is in this book. I have read it twice. I have sought
the bird from Berkeley Square (where I cannot believe it ever
sang) through the lanes of Kent to the downs of Wiltshire,
yet never been fully sure it was a nightingale I heard. I have
studied it in recordings and plunged into Edward Armstrong's
masterpiece on birdsong. I am *almost* an expert.

Why the nightingale? Why not the lark or the thrush, the

robin or the blackbird? Mr Mabey has no doubt, nor had John Clare in the passage quoted above. The 'carefree fluency' of its song is unrivalled in ornithology and offers poets a ready contrast to the melancholy of daily life. The nightingale arrives in Britain each April from Africa. Once here it throws back its head and sends into the spring air a burst of spondees, gradually rising in tempo until they shatter into a thousand pieces. To H. E. Bates the noise conveyed a 'sense of breath-lessness and restraint, of restraint about to be broken . . . a sort of tuning up, then flaring out in a moment into a cres-cendo of fire and honey.'

By 1650 scholars were already trying to capture nightingale song in written notation. Musicians have been trying ever since. Modern recording has revealed the depth of the diffi-culty. Computers have analysed birdsong into as many as 150 separate notes a second. A momentary chord of a nightingale becomes an ultrasonic symphony of harmonies and percuss-ives, glissandi and tutti. The composer David Hindley has delved into these chords and found in them perfect musical formations. A nightingale's vocal equipment can produce four distinct notes at once, and with its mouth shut. Has all of nature a more astonishing creation than the larynx of a nightingale?

To the medieval troubadours, the nightingale's song, the insistent intervals leading to a frantic tumble of notes, was full of sexual connotation. In parts of Italy, 'hearing the night-ingales sing' (*ludir cantar l'usinguolo*, wrote Boccaccio) remains a euphemism for sex. Always the bird has been a symbol of spring and of romance. Dryden 'stood entranced and had no room for thought/But all o'erpowered with ecstasy of bliss'. The bird's annual arrival on these shores was God's affirmation of rebirth.

To the Romantics the nightingale was irresistible. Shelley declared: 'Sounds overflow the listener's brain/So sweet, that joy is almost pain.' Keats had only to hear one that 'singest of summer with full-throated ease' and imagine it retreating across Hampstead Heath, beckoning him to follow. So intense was the inspiration that he sat under the tree in Fanny

Brawne's garden and wrote his ode in just three hours. 'Now more than ever seems it rich to die . . . While thou art pouring forth thy soul abroad/In such an ecstasy.'

From Pliny and Ovid to Milton and Blake, the nightingale's call has been insistent and compelling. Cecil Sharp found identical songs being sung about nightingales in places as far apart as Somerset and the southern Appalachians, carried from the one to the other by settlers over three centuries. 'Hark, hark said the fair maid, how the nightingales do sing,' ran the lyric. Not to be left out, the Metropolitan Railway Company advertised its new estates as 'blessed with the song of nightingales'. In Metroland these birds 'render Rickmansworth a Mecca to the City man pining for country'.

Nightingale song is, like most birdsong, primarily about territory, though some observers have decided that younger nightingales seem to sing for the sheer joy of it. The song is performed by the male while the female builds the nest and incubates the eggs. Mr Mabey watched one bird sing its heart out while its mouth was full of food brought to feed its young. An ornithologist reported in 1929, 'I have never seen a bird so brimful of emotion. Each time he visited his brooding mate he sang such a song as I have never heard before.' Its mouth too was full at the time. There must be a lesson here for the Royal Opera House canteen.

Another ornithologist, named Montagu, discovered in 1802 that when the female was removed from the nest, the male sang even louder. He pointed out that birdsong was not merely territorial but crucial to species identification for mating. Armstrong even discussed whether nightingales sing in local dialect. Some claim to be able to detect regional variants, but he could see no difference between a Nottinghamshire nightingale and one heard in the Camargue. I should have thought every nightingale musically unique, like every soprano, though digital computers may yet detect regional differences.

Certainly nightingales can be trained. Berlin zoologists once captured two pairs and were able to teach them up to 60 different musical phrases. As for endurance, the nightingale is phenomenal. One has been recorded singing continuously for five hours and 25 minutes without a moment's pause. The record is reputedly 23 hours 30 minutes in one day. Whether other birds can beat that I do not know. The *Guinness Book of Records* is silent on the matter.

Mr Mabey confronts head-on the Great Nightingale Dilemma, whether its song should be regarded as joyful or melancholic. Is it the mournful dryad of the trees, seducing Keats to an early death? Or was Coleridge right to deride such a view as of 'some night-wandering man whose heart was pierced with the remembrance of a grievous wrong, or slow distemper or neglected love'? To him the nightingale was merry and capricious. It 'crowds and hurries and precipitates with fast thick warbles his delicious notes.' It lets its 'liquid siftings fall' on Agamemnon's bloody wood in T. S. Eliot's *Sweeney Among the Nightingales*. It is a bird of happiness.

I am with Coleridge. These birds seem to be ever cheerful. They are known to sing in the most trying circumstances. They start up at the sound of thunder and continue through heavy storms and even gunfire. There are many mentions of them singing in the Great War trenches, bringing the delicious music of the hedgerows to homesick soldiers. Nor are they averse to showbusiness. The Second World War gave the nightingale its biggest audience. The cellist Beatrice Harrison had found a nightingale singing alone with her when she was practising in her garden. In 1924 she suggested that the BBC attempt to broadcast their duet.

Lord Reith opposed the plan on the grounds that 'tinned nightingale' would stop people going out into the woods and lanes for themselves. It would also kill conversation, a quaint objection from the head of a radio station. But the experiment went ahead. The BBC's first outside broadcast was of a nightingale, from a coppice in Miss Harrison's garden. The concert was held annually for 18 years. Only when the bird and cello found themselves competing with an overhead bomber did the War Ministry declare the broadcast a breach of security and stop the transmission. This last duet, of nightingale and bomber, ecstasy and death, was none the less secretly recorded. Today the tape is a classic of broadcasting history.

Like many species the nightingale is on the wane. Perhaps it is succumbing to the current plague of the magpie and the sparrow hawk. Mr Mabey reports that nightingales are present in large numbers only in Suffolk, Essex and Kent. From tens of thousands of pairs estimated to have summered in Britain in the 1950s, probably no more than 2,000 are still arriving today. The best hope for them lies in the return of arable land to scrub and coppiced woodland.

I am no ornithologist but know enough of birds to regard them as the most entrancing of creatures. Small wonder the Hindus used to think of them as the highest form of life, above even humans. They could sing and fly. Their vast global migrations are still the bafflement of science. They seem to possess a secret of the earth and sky that is denied to man. The survival of each species is a measure of the world's ecological balance. All birds are beautiful, without equal in nature both in sight and sound. The most beautiful in sound is the nightingale.

Its song is not, as Mr Mabey says, a mere way-station on some evolutionary road. This is no preliminary to a greater perfection, not nature's first stab at Bach or Schubert or the soprano voice. The nightingale's song is pure music, a complete and finished thing, different from the human voice in every way. It is, says Mabey, 'an example of the mysterious emergence of beauty from matter'. It cannot be extinguished.

INDEX

223